NIGHTS BELOW FOORD STREET

Nights below Foord Street

Literature and Popular Culture in Postindustrial Nova Scotia

PETER THOMPSON

McGill-Queen's University Press
Montreal & Kingston • London • Chicago

© McGill-Queen's University Press 2019

ISBN 978-0-7735-5933-2 (cloth)
ISBN 978-0-7735-5934-9 (paper)
ISBN 978-0-2280-0052-5 (ePDF)
ISBN 978-0-2280-0053-2 (ePUB)

Legal deposit fourth quarter 2019
Bibliothèque nationale du Québec

Printed in Canada on acid-free paper that is 100% ancient forest free (100% post-consumer recycled), processed chlorine free

This book has been published with the help of a grant from the Canadian Federation for the Humanities and Social Sciences, through the Awards to Scholarly Publications Program, using funds provided by the Social Sciences and Humanities Research Council of Canada.

We acknowledge the support of the Canada Council for the Arts.

Nous remercions le Conseil des arts du Canada de son soutien.

Library and Archives Canada Cataloguing in Publication

Title: Nights below Foord Street: literature and popular culture in postindustrial Nova Scotia / Peter Thompson.

Names: Thompson, Peter, 1981– author.

Description: Includes bibliographical references and index.

Identifiers: Canadiana (print) 2019019829X | Canadiana (ebook) 20190198435 | ISBN 9780773559349 (paper) | ISBN 9780773559332 (cloth) | ISBN 9780228000525 (ePDF) | ISBN 9780228000532 (ePUB)

Subjects: LCSH: Canadian literature—Nova Scotia—History and criticism. | LCSH: Canadian literature—21st century—History and criticism. | LCSH: Popular culture—Nova Scotia. | LCSH: Deindustrialization—Nova Scotia. | LCSH: Nova Scotia—In popular culture. | CSH: Canadian literature (English)—Nova Scotia—History and criticism. | CSH: Canadian literature (English)—21st century—History and criticism.

Classification: LCC PS8131.N6 T56 2019 | DDC C810.9/9716—dc23

This book was typeset by Marquis Interscript in 11/14 Sabon.

For R. Mark Hamilton

Contents

Figures ix

Acknowledgments xi

Introduction 3

1 The Industrial Era 25

2 Cultures of Extraction in Northern Nova Scotia 48

3 Masculine Anxieties in Postindustrial Nova Scotia 70

4 Trash the Kilt: Whiteness in Post-Tartan Nova Scotia 92

5 *Cottonland* and *Oxyana*: Prescription Drugs and Moral Panics 118

6 Conclusion: *What Remains* 137

Notes 145

Works Cited 151

Index 167

Figures

I.1 Demolition of Westray silos, 27 November 1998. Norman Munro Collection. Image courtesy of Pictou-Antigonish Regional Library. 4

I.2 Westray site, 22 May 1992. Norman Munro Collection. Image courtesy of Pictou-Antigonish Regional Library. 5

I.3 Springhill welcome sign. Photo by Peter Thompson. 8

1.1 Kate Beaton, "East Coast Literature." Comic sketch. www.harkavagrant.com 41

2.1 Novelty hard hats, Springhill Miners' Museum. Photo by Peter Thompson. 53

5.1 Roseland Cabaret, 12 October 2013. Image courtesy of *The News*. 120

6.1 Eliot Wright, *Pioneer Coal Mine (II), Stellarton NS, 2013*, from the series *What Remains* (2013–14). 139

6.2 Eliot Wright, *Nova Forge (I), Trenton NS, 2013*, from the series *What Remains* (2013–14). 140

6.3 Liz Wright, *Coal*, from the series *What Remains* (2013–14). Coal, bronze, sterling silver, pyrite, yellowheart, black onyx. Photo by Eliot Wright. 141

6.4 Liz Wright, *Forge*, from the series *What Remains* (2013–14). Ostrich feather, sterling silver, copper, steel, Nova Forge brick. Photo by Eliot Wright. 142

Acknowledgments

I read Leo McKay's *Like This* when I was in high school and David Adams Richards's *Nights below Station Street* when I was in third year at St Francis Xavier University. My interest in Atlantic Canadian literature comes directly out of those two moments, so I'm happy to pay homage to McKay and Richards in the title of this book.

I'm not sure what I ever did to deserve it, but I have a very full life surrounded by generous and thoughtful people, all of whom did much to help this project along. I want to thank my long list of mentors, including Mary McGillivray, Peter Twohig, Tony Tremblay, Gwendolyn Davies, Michèle Lacombe, Parker Duchemin, André Loiselle, Pauline Rankin, and the late Herb Wyile.

I was hired at Carleton University during a massive generational shift in the Faculty of Arts and Social Sciences; thus, I've spent the early part of my career in a dynamic, challenging, and fun environment that pushed me to develop many of these ideas. I'm leaving many people out, but I especially want to thank friends and colleagues Peter Hodgins, Jennifer Adese, Jurek Elzanowski, and Tim Di Leo Browne (a special thanks to Tim for the many drives on I-81 to the Appalachian Studies Association conference, trips that shaped this book in all kinds of ways). Thanks to Donna Malone and Lori Dearman for their expertise in all administrative matters and for making the twelfth floor of Dunton Tower such a great place to spend my days.

I was lucky enough to have the opportunity to present this research at conferences around the world as the project unfolded.

I received valuable input in all of these venues. This book would not have been possible, however, without the collegial and hilariously sharp group of Atlantic Canadianists that's coalesced at the Atlantic Canada Studies and Thomas Raddall conferences over this decade. I owe a particular thank you to Alexander MacLeod and Paul Chafe for their collaboration and friendship over the years.

Parts of chapter 2 and chapter 4 appeared in different forms in *Journal of Canadian Studies* 49, no. 1 (2015) and *Studies in Canadian Literature* 37, no. 2 (2013) respectively. Thank you to the editors of these journals for permission to reprint this material here. Thanks to Kate Beaton, Eliot Wright, and Liz Wright for their fantastic work and for generously allowing me include it. I appreciate the efforts of Greg Hayward at the Pictou-Antigonish Regional Library, Erika Smith at the Nova Scotia Museum of Industry, and Adam MacInnis at *The News* in tracking down several images.

It's been a pleasure to work with McGill-Queen's University Press on this project. Kyla Madden's wisdom, patience, and eminently kind email persona made this long process smooth and pleasant. Thanks to Finn Purcell, Kathleen Fraser, Filomena Falocco, Lisa Aitken, and Kate Merriman for their essential behind-the-scenes work in getting the book ready for publication. I'm both proud and humbled to publish with MQUP, a press that has produced many of the most important titles in the field of Atlantic Canada Studies – books that in some cases changed my life. I am indebted to MQUP's two anonymous readers, both of whom engaged seriously with the manuscript and offered the kind of substantial and meaningful feedback you hope for when entering into peer review. Their hard work and constructive suggestions made this book much stronger.

I want to thank my parents, Kathy and Leonard, my brothers and sisters, Casey and Marie Rocznik, Patty Field, Paul and Ronda White, and my friends in Ottawa, Halifax, and Pictou County for their love, support, and good humour. I'd also like to take the opportunity to remember my grandfather, Peter White, whose stories about his father travelling to Kentucky for mining safety courses sparked my interest in connections between the Nova Scotian and Appalachian coalfields, and my grandmother, Mary

Thompson, whose cupboards shook in Plymouth on the morning of the Westray explosion.

I wrote a lot of what follows in coffee shops during my sabbatical in 2015–16. Thanks very much to the staff at the various downtown Ottawa Bridgeheads for feeding me and allowing me to loiter.

I picked away at this book for five years. During that time, my family expanded dramatically. My final thanks go to the three most important people: my wife, Andy, my daughter, Hanna, and my son, Quinn Hong. Thanks for putting up with me, for cheering me on, and for always being there for Friday movie nights. I'm incredibly lucky.

NIGHTS BELOW FOORD STREET

And if we get lost we can find out
Where it was we used to be
We're following signs to the sea
So take your time if you're leaving before me
Sloan, "The N.S."

Introduction

I grew up in a small town called Stellarton on Nova Scotia's North Shore. When I was a teenager, I spent most of my time talking incessantly about TV and movies with my friends and dreaming about the day I would finally be able to leave to go to university. Despite my best efforts to ignore the goings-on in my hometown, the unique set of political and cultural tensions playing out in Stellarton in the late 1990s stayed with me and ultimately inspired this project. While I was busy with reruns of *Seinfeld* and *The Simpsons*, local politicians and business types were fighting to keep the province's coal mines, steel plants, and manufacturing base alive. Stellarton eventually witnessed a nasty, bare-knuckles version of the postindustrial economy emerge. The shift was immediately palpable: jobs in the industrial sector disappeared, call centres moved in, local community colleges launched degrees in tourism and hospitality, and many of my classmates and family members moved west to find work.

Three moments stand out: the 1992 Westray mine disaster, which took place less than two kilometres from my childhood home; an extended fight in the mid-1990s between environmentalists and Pioneer Coal over a strip mine the company wanted to build directly in my neighbourhood (I'll let you guess who won); and the ceremonial demolition of the distinctive Westray silos in 1998. The last event is clearest in my mind. On the day it happened, my teacher escorted our class to a park at the top of a nearby hill so that we could watch in confused silence as the silos collapsed across

I.I Demolition of Westray silos, 27 November 1998

I.2 Westray site, 22 May 1992

the river from my school. This moment was a key inspiration for Leo McKay's *Twenty-Six* (2003) and was designed to send a message to the residents of northern Nova Scotia that the industrial era was completely over, that the social and environmental damage from the Westray disaster had been repaired, and that we were on the cusp of a new economic era, one that would move the province past the dangers and inconveniences of digging resources out of the ground.

This book is my attempt to understand Nova Scotia's struggle to come to terms with its extractive and industrial past, which includes a legacy of overexploitation of the natural environment, lingering problems with pollution, intermittent disasters, and labour violence. More specifically, I investigate the ways in which the province's contemporary authors and film and television-makers challenge the romantic and nostalgic portrait of Nova Scotia's industrial heritage promoted in museums, monuments, tourist sites, and other places. This book is an interdisciplinary examination of postindustrial Nova Scotia's literary texts (Lynn Coady, Leo McKay, Sarah Mian, Jonathan Campbell), television (*Trailer Park Boys*), film (*Blackbird, Cottonland, Poor Boy's Game*), and heritage sites (Nova Scotia Museum of Industry, Cape Breton Miners' Museum, Springhill Miners' Museum). What emerges is a contested and contradictory narrative of change in this region: on the one hand, the state and the tourism industry push a story of progress and a clean break between the industrial era and the postindustrial era, and on the other, the authors and artists I examine depict a messy and unfinished process in which industrial and extractive activities died a slow death, leaving behind a polluted and denatured landscape and new ways of exploiting the region's inhabitants.

***

In November 2001, news stories popped up across Nova Scotia and other parts of Canada heralding the end of the age of coal in industrial Cape Breton. In a typical piece, "The Era of Coal Mining in Atlantic Canada Ends," the *Guelph Daily Mercury* reported, "a 280-year-old way of life ended with little fanfare Friday as miners removed the final piece of coal from the last Cape Breton colliery" (Canadian Press 2001, D07). These stories share a common structure. They touch briefly on the long, proud history of coal mining in northern Nova Scotia and the way in which this industry sustained families and communities for generations. They go on to express uncertainty about what lies ahead and to emphasize the hardship awaiting these places as they transition to a new way of life. Crucially, however, these articles always end on a hopeful note: they point to the dawn of a new economic era in which the service industry will transform and modernize the province. Many specifically reference call centres, which all levels of government pitched in to subsidize in the wake of the closure of the Cape Breton Development Corporation (DEVCO) and the

Sydney Steel Corporation (SYSCO) at the turn of the century.[1] This narrative structure – based on a sharp transition from the industrial era to the postindustrial era – is possible because of a series of events that took place in Nova Scotia at the end of the 1990s: the fallout from the Westray inquiry, the unveiling of the Nova Scotia Museum of Industry, the collapse of industrial Cape Breton, the retraining of miners to work in call centres and in demonstration mines, and the optimistic predictions about ending the boom and bust cycles of the old industries and capitalizing on the promise of tourism and other service-based ventures. The narrative the province and the media pushed was that Nova Scotia's dirty, dangerous, and unsustainable industrial economy had to be replaced by a modern, efficient workforce, one that could build on the strengths of the province's education system and culture of hospitality and, in the oft-repeated words of politicians both local and national, transition the province into a new era.

This moment speaks to a key tension in contemporary Nova Scotia: the clash between the push to "move forward" and the stubborn refusal of the past to be sanitized and cleaned away. As much as Nova Scotia was and is, in the words of Ian McKay and Robin Bates, the "province of history," the idea of moving forward is also a recurring motif in its political discourse and public space. This is especially true in the province's former mining areas: Pictou County's slogan is "Forward Together," and Springhill's (printed on a sign shaped like a piece of coal) is "from our mining past to a greener future."[2]

One of the ways that the province secures this recurrent narrative of progress is by controlling the message surrounding its industrial heritage. Much of rural Nova Scotia's economy was built around extracting fish, lumber, and coal. In places like Pictou and Sydney, industrial development in the form of fish-processing plants, pulp and paper mills, and steel mills took place to support these activities (Summerby-Murray 2015, 70). Over the past fifty years, the region has undergone a steady process of deindustrialization in which many of these mills and mines closed. As this took place, the province turned to its industrial past to form much of its tourism and heritage infrastructure: visitors can marvel at the

I.3 Springhill welcome sign

unbelievable range of products built in twentieth-century Nova Scotia at the Museum of Industry in Stellarton, tour mine sites in Springhill and Glace Bay, and pan for gold at Ovens Natural Park in Lunenburg County.

Nova Scotia's relationship with resource extraction is complicated by the position it occupies in the province's cultural memory. Coal mining, for example, is memorialized through songs, stories, museums, named highways, monuments, and plaques. Transient workers from the province travel offshore and to Alberta to participate in energy megaprojects and politicians continue to tout resource extraction as a potential future solution to the region's economic problems. The persistence of the extractive model – consider, for example, strip-mining projects in Westville and Stellarton, continued efforts to open and sustain mines in Cape Breton, and even the tourist economy, which is built on extracting a certain kind of cultural experience before moving on – is only one indication of the province's reluctance to "move forward" from the industrial era.

This book is about the lingering effects of the industrial era – its physical remnants, its way of viewing the natural environment, and the kinds of social relationships it fostered – and the complicated role these objects and ideas play in the province's cultural identity. I attempt to recast this narrative about the shift to the postindustrial era at the end of the 1990s and to think about the things left behind by the industrial economy, including pollution, ideas about the working-class body, anxieties surrounding masculinity, and forms of drug addiction and substance abuse.

APPROACHING ATLANTIC CANADA: A NOTE ON R.M. VAUGHAN

My study is an addition to a body of scholarship on Atlantic Canadian literature and popular culture that has grown exponentially over the past decade and a half. Since the turn of the century, a wide range of writers, cultural producers, and scholars have challenged stereotypes about the region and reoriented what we know about its cultural traditions.

Critics working on contemporary Atlantic Canadian literature and film argue that one of the major challenges cultural producers face is the set of long-standing assumptions about what counts as regional culture. Tony Tremblay, for example, has argued that reviewers, academics, and members of the literary establishment from central Canada often push the idea that Atlantic Canadian culture is conservative or sentimental. He writes, "If professional readers are to be believed, our literature has become a heritage tourism industry, the subtexts of which use myth extradiagetically to consolidate power in recognizably colonial ways" (Tremblay 2008, 30). These standards, he suggests, demand that writers conform to narrow parameters that privilege romantic depictions of a region steeped in history, lost in time, and home to a backward cast of easily recognizable characters.

While these forces clearly have a significant impact on the kind of literature and culture that is produced – and, critically, published

– in the region, other writers, such as Herb Wyile, flip this dynamic around, pointing out that since the turn of the century, Atlantic Canadian writers and cultural producers have parlayed their profound irritation with this "official" version of culture into an ironic and often subversive reimagining of these entrenched myths and stereotypes (Coady 2003; Ivison 2011; Wyile and Lynes 2008; Wyile 2011).

In what follows, I suggest that the popular culture and literature of postindustrial Nova Scotia reveals the tension between stereotypes about the province and the rest of the region and social cleavages such as outmigration, overexploitation of natural resources, the persistence of racism, the crisis of masculinity, and environmental degradation. One of the consequences of the push for tourism in the province is that it leads to a romantic and nostalgic reading of many of these concepts. The romantic version of Nova Scotia recasts outmigration as evidence of a footloose and adventurous (Scottish) culture (McKay and Bates 2010, 309), regressive ideas about gender as the persistence of the strong Maritime family, and even racism, homophobia, and antienvironmentalism as down-home conservatism and loyalty to tradition.

There are three significant moments that set the stage for the shift that Wyile identifies. The first is the publication in the 1970s of regionalist studies in political economy and history – all of which challenged a nationalist framework that attributed economic downturn in Atlantic Canada to an inherently conservative and almost workshy[3] culture in the region, an assessment perhaps best exemplified by Stephen Harper's 2002 comments about Atlantic Canada's "culture of defeat" (Laghi 2002). Studies on Atlantic Canadian literature in the 1980s and 1990s employed this approach widely, leading to a connection between the region's literary criticism and political economy that persists to this day. These studies suggest that during this time, regional presses emerged, authors and critics alike became ambivalent about the nationalist project of the 1960s, and writers began to critique the spatial and political logic of Canada's federation and forces that marginalized writers from the region (Armstrong and Wyile 1997; Atherton 1984; Cogswell 1985; Kulyk Keefer 1987; Lochhead 1985; Seaman 1976). Gwendolyn

Davies' studies – *Studies in Maritime Literary History* (1991) and *Myth and Milieu: Atlantic Literature and Culture* (1993) – laid much of the groundwork for the more critical and cultural studies-inflected work currently taking place in Atlantic Canada Studies. She links the political and economic circumstances of the region to the region's literary history, noting that authors internalized these periods of unrest and that they in turn fuelled its literary history. Davies suggests that one of the most powerful symbols in Maritime writing is the home place. She argues that "from the 1920s onward, the 'home place' emerges as a symbol of cultural continuity and psychological identification in the face of social fragmentation, outmigration, and a continuing hardscrabble economy" (*Studies in Maritime Literary History*, 194).[4]

The second development that shapes contemporary Atlantic Canadian literary and cultural criticism is the explosion of cultural production in Newfoundland. Flowing out of the success of the Burning Rock Collective, contemporary Newfoundland literature demands cutting-edge critical tools, constructs St John's as a cosmopolitan and complex urban space, and challenges much of what we think we know about the culture of Eastern Canada (Armstrong 2010; Chafe 2008; Delisle 2013; Mathews 2004; Wyile and Lynes 2008). Newfoundland literature is in a massive upswing, as award-winning authors such as Jessica Grant, Michael Winter, Kathleen Winter, and Lisa Moore continue to push its boundaries. In turn, this dramatic expansion of cultural output has led to an increase in the scope, quality, quantity, and theoretical sophistication of Atlantic Canadian literary criticism over the past ten to fifteen years.

This renaissance in Atlantic Canadian literary criticism is heavily influenced by theoretical work in the field of spatial identity theory – particularly the work of Henri Lefebvre, Edward Soja, Doreen Massey, and David Jordan – which sees space as a social construct; narratives about regions and people who inhabit them are produced and contested for political purposes, and the state and corporate interests mobilize versions of regional identity in ways that distort lived experience and suppress political movements.[5] In the case of Atlantic Canada, this observation goes a long way toward explaining the outsized role of tourism in the region. In the opening pages of *Anne of Tim Hortons: Globalization and the Reshaping of Atlantic-Canadian Literature*, Wyile acknowledges the impact that this body of literature has had on Atlantic Canadian literary criticism: "region is increasingly being viewed not as a geographical/cultural/political given but as a construct, a kind of imagined and at times strategic sense of cohesion and community, projected usually from without but sometimes also from within" (Wyile 2011, 8). Thus, the concept of region itself is a hotly contested idea in Atlantic Canadian literary and cultural criticism. Recent scholarship in this area moves beyond the idea that Atlantic Canadian regionalism is a counternarrative to nationalist culture in Canada and questions the idea that the region is home to a uniform culture. My approach in this book is similar in spirit and I am indebted to the work of earlier critics who theorize and problematize the concept of region.

It's impossible to write a book on the culture of Nova Scotia without acknowledging the third – and arguably most important – moment: the publication in 1994 of Ian McKay's highly influential *The Quest of the Folk: Antimodernism and Cultural Selection in Twentieth-Century Nova Scotia*. *The Quest of the Folk* was a groundbreaking study that examined the province's carefully planned push to define itself as a place removed from the stresses of modern life in the middle of the twentieth century. The impact of *The Quest of the Folk* on the study of Atlantic Canadian literature and popular culture is difficult to overstate. For the past twenty years, critics have been obsessed with the impact of the tourism industry, and its branding of the region as quaint and hospitable, on the development of Atlantic Canadian literature and popular culture. The influence of McKay's work is evident throughout the study of heritage, literature, popular culture, and architecture in Atlantic Canada, as scholars examine the impact of stereotypes, the tourism industry, and questions over land ownership, work, ethnicity, and tradition.[6]

Critics such as Wyile and David Creelman argue that the key issue for the current generation of contemporary Atlantic cultural producers is negotiating entrenched ideas about "the folk." In one of the most important statements in contemporary Atlantic

Canadian literary criticism, Creelman suggests in *Setting in the East: Maritime Realist Fiction* (2003) that, "If there is a common ethos in the Maritimes it lies not in a 'sense of shared community' but in the *memory* of a shared community" (Creelman 2003, 11). In *Anne of Tim Hortons: Globalization and the Reshaping of Atlantic-Canadian Literature* (2011), a study that is both highly influential and particularly indebted to *The Quest of the Folk*, Wyile argues that contemporary Atlantic Canadian literature and popular culture is marked by ambivalence toward earlier nostalgic accounts of the region and the "folk paradigm" (Wyile 2011, 21) – the assumption that the region is backward, innocent, welcoming to tourists, and picturesque. Instead, contemporary Atlantic Canadian cultural producers construct a region that is immersed in North American mass culture and widely impacted by neoliberal approaches to economics and patterns of work.[7]

I come back to McKay and Wyile's indispensable concept of the folk paradigm in almost every chapter, but for now I want to frame my discussion of the culture of postindustrial Nova Scotia in slightly different terms. In a short and seldom-cited article published in *Semiotext(e)* in 1994, R.M. Vaughan submits a scathing assessment of the way images of Atlantic Canada fit into the country's mainstream culture. The east coast, he argues, is trapped in a "colonial double-bind" in which it is associated largely with outmoded images of a region dependent on resource extraction and bound to the earth and sea. This romanticized past defines residents of the region, even though the activities and practices it evokes are no longer a meaningful part of day-to-day life. For Vaughan, "the people who live [in Atlantic Canada] have provided [central Canada] with a key mythology in the narrative of nation building – the mystery of the folk [and] the feudal drama of an early 'homeland' people who mark the beginning of the time line of progress" (Vaughan 1994, 169). Vaughan argues that many of the images associated with Atlantic Canada – the lobster, the grizzled fisherman, the lighthouse, to name a few[8] – symbolize obsolescence and servitude. But they serve a practical function within the logic of Canadian nationalism: by reinforcing the idea that the region is in constant decline and perpetually with its hand out, stereotypes about Atlantic Canada help to create a pool of cheap labour and a store of exploitable resources, which crucially include cultural resources, for the rest of the country.

Vaughan's article is worth revisiting because he provides a framework for thinking about representations of Atlantic Canada in a world where the descendants of McKay's elusive folk, as represented in contemporary Nova Scotian literature and popular culture, are out of work, addicted to oxycontin, listening to ac/dc, and eating buckets of Kentucky Fried Chicken. While McKay and Wyile talk about an active process of cultural formation, appropriation, and ironic subversion, Vaughan argues that the state, corporate interests, and cultural producers mine these stereotypes until they are stripped of any meaning. Vaughan makes a connection between the aggressive overexploitation of the landscape and the equally aggressive overexploitation of the region's culture: for him, the folk paradigm is not produced so much as it is left behind and picked over, much like the region's natural resources. He argues that regional stereotypes in Atlantic Canada lead to a process of infantilization in which residents of the region are dysfunctional, unable to participate helpfully in the national project (unless they are leaving and exploiting resources elsewhere), and always expected to be at the ready for visitors looking for "authentic" cultural experiences. This book examines the ambivalent response to this situation crafted by postindustrial Nova Scotia's contemporary literature and popular culture.

A NOTE ON TERMINOLOGY

While each chapter deals with a different aspect of contemporary Nova Scotia's response to the shift away from the industrial and extractive era, there are three core ideas to which I continually return: postindustrial, extraction, and the body.

Postindustrial

Deindustrialization – in the classic definition proposed by Barry Bluestone and Bennett Harrison, "a widespread, systematic disinvestment in the nation's basic productive capacity" (Bluestone and

Harrison 1982, 6) – has a range of economic and cultural impacts (High and Lewis 2007, 2). In *Beyond the Ruins: The Meanings of Deindustrialization* (2003), Jefferson Cowie and Joseph Heathcott suggest that in addition to exploring the devastating impact deindustrialization has on the livelihood of people living in places such as Detroit, Sudbury, and Sydney, scholars also need to attend to its spatial transformations, its penchant for inspiring nostalgia, and to the ways politicians and business elites employ this term. For them, the term "postindustrial" is misleading, as the West's manufacturing and industrial base has simply moved to other parts of the world (rather than disappeared); furthermore, they argue that many of the social, cultural, and economic organizing principles of the industrial era persist.

This book builds on this observation: I suggest that the *perception* that Nova Scotia has entered a postindustrial era is just as important as the material and social effects of deindustrialization. This perception and the narrative that emerges from it are sustained in several ways. In *Corporate Wasteland: The Landscape and Memory of Deindustrialization* (2007), Steven High contends that the ceremonial destruction of grain elevators and factories as well as the elaborate process of turning these spaces into tourist attractions and condominiums contributes to the idea that the postindustrial era is both transformative and permanent; he writes, "The repetition of this secular ritual across North America – and the diffusion of these dramatic images in the media – reinforces the sense of inevitability surrounding industrial decline" (High and Lewis 2007, 10). Of course, the term *post*-industrial is a slippery one, since Nova Scotia continues to subsidize various extractive activities, is home to clear-cutting projects, and works toward keeping a conventional mine open in Donkin. The term "postindustrial" is useful in this analysis because it captures this ambivalence: although we think of the extractive economy as a thing of the past, coal mining continues to resonate as a powerful marker of identity in northern Nova Scotia and the physical impacts of the industry are still very much present. As a quick example, the popular reality television show *The Curse of Oak Island* embodies the province's contradictory relationship with extractive capitalism.

On the surface, the show is about two brothers, Rick and Marty Lagina, who purchase and operate a tour company, Oak Island Adventures, and who attempt to solve a centuries-old mystery. At the same time, the show presents the quest inspired by Oak Island's legend as a straightforward excavation project: the brothers rely on their expertise from the natural gas industry, they use the latest in extractive techniques, and in later seasons, they even partner with Irving to try to extract the buried treasure. These cultural products demonstrate that the "post" in postindustrial is unresolved. As much as the media and the tourism industry portray these activities as part of the past, and the province's memorial complex looks to construct a narrative of rehabilitation, this is just a story: the things left over from the industrial era continue to form a key part of the province's cultural and physical landscape.

In what follows, I examine this idea from a number of angles. In addition to the material effects of the pullout of industries and extractive projects, Nova Scotia is also shaped by this narrative of decline; politicians, businesses, and the tourism industry all use this story to serve their own ends (Linkon 2013, 38; Wyile 2011, 148). The fall of the industrial era – which appears to be inevitable and which throws these communities into chaos – ups the ante on further economic development: for example, people who protest environmental calamities like Boat Harbour hear that this kind of pollution is necessary to keep jobs in the region (Andreatta 2013). In this way, postindustrial Nova Scotia is, to use Rebecca Scott's language in describing the Appalachian coalfield, "a place that can only save itself by destroying itself: inasmuch as it remains unsacrificed, it does not achieve national belonging" (Scott 2010, 222). As is the case in many parts of North America, this logic makes the rise of the prison industry in northern Nova Scotia an important part of the shift to the postindustrial era. Many of the cultural texts I discuss engage with tensions around the criminalization of the province's working class and with anxieties about incarceration. In 2010, there was a wide public debate over where Nova Scotia should build its new prison; unsurprisingly, the two areas that were vying for the prison on the basis that it would provide jobs in a depressed economy were the former mining regions of Springhill and Pictou County (cbc 2010).[9]

As many of the texts I discuss in the book demonstrate, postindustrial Nova Scotia embodies Scott's paradox. The tourism industry touts the province and in particular much of northern Nova Scotia (including Pictou County and Cape Breton) as a destination on the basis of its beautiful landscape, but the province is dotted with sites like Northern Pulp[10] and the Pioneer strip mine that complicate the idea that the province is "postindustrial" and demonstrate that the connection between Nova Scotia's culture and ideas about resource extraction continues to resonate. Thus, the starting point of this book is the material impacts of this confusion about whether or not the province has entered a "postindustrial" era and the way in which authors and cultural producers represent this story's messy fallout.

Extraction

The continued emphasis on dragging things out of the ground in Nova Scotia's "postindustrial" era leads me to the book's second conceptual signpost: extraction. Northern Nova Scotia is often positioned as what Henri Lefebvre has called an "abstract" space (Edensor 2005, 8) that exists to be exploited, in the past for its abundant natural resources, but today for its distinctive traditions. This emphasis on extraction might help to explain the region's ambivalent relationship with nature (governments and corporations in the region still search for new and inventive ways of extracting things from the environment, such as offshore oil exploration and strip mining) and with culture (in a world in which primary industries have failed, residents of the region sell a watered-down and a-critical version of their history, including the history of the resource economy).

In his work on the environmental and social impact of mining in Australia, Ghassan Hage points out that contemporary capitalism is wrapped up with various forms of extraction. While our reliance on the extraction of minerals or other materials is the most obvious example, Hage explains that extraction is also a key element of the knowledge economy and modern policing: for instance, companies extract information about consumers and their spending habits from websites, doctors and investigators extract dna and other biological identity-markers from patients and suspects, and the cia and other security operations extract information from detainees through interrogations and other measures. Hage argues that the modern global economy relies on what he calls "cultures of extraction" that teach us to constantly look for new ways to "capture what exists with and along us and [transform] it into something that exists for us" (Hage 2011, 5).

In her 2007 book *Bringing Down the Mountains*, Shirley Stewart Burns observes that the transformation of spaces impacted by excessive resource extraction takes place in three stages: exploration, extraction, and reclamation. Reclamation refers to the physical remediation of the landscape, which may involve planting trees, reseeding fields, or urban renewal projects such as building parks and ball diamonds. But the reclamation process also involves a spiritual or cultural renewal that takes the form of memorializing disasters and labour disputes, creating a tourism infrastructure, and pushing the idea that these communities have moved beyond the industrial era and into a new, clean, and efficient postindustrial economy. In Nova Scotia, examples of this logic at work include the 2013 contest to have school children rename the Sydney Tar Ponds and the construction of parks on strip-mined areas in Westville and Stellarton. This narrative is possible, she argues, in part because of the key role that activities such as mining play in collective memory – common phrases include "we are shaped by coal" or "we have coal in the blood" – and because the extraction of coal and other resources is often framed as an expression of nationalism.

In his essay "Ideas of Nature," however, Raymond Williams suggests that the byproducts of the industrial era complicate this kind of logic. For Williams, the idea that we can map, survey, and separate the physical world into abstract spaces, take what we want from it, and then smooth over these actions overlooks the impact of the traces and scars of what he calls modern industrial society's "operations on nature" (Williams 1980, 80). Williams argues that although we tend to think of extraction as removing something and cleanly taking it away, an equally important part of this process is the material that is left over. We think of strip mining, to continue using this example, as an activity that produces coal and electricity and the resulting piles of dirt, tailings, and clay as byproducts; however, this excess material is just as important as the objects taken out of the ground. Williams writes, "In our complex dealings with the physical world, we find it very difficult to recognize all the products of our own activities. We recognize some of the products, and call others by-products; but the slagheap is as real a product as the coal, just as the river stinking with sewage and detergent is as much our product as the reservoir ... Furthermore, we ourselves are in a sense products: the pollution of industrial society is to be found not only in the water and in the air but in the slums, the traffic jams, and not these only as physical objects but as ourselves in them and in relation to them" (Williams 1980, 83). Williams argues that contemporary capitalism proceeds by pushing these extractive activities to the periphery, selectively ignoring the unsightly or inconvenient material produced by them, and constructing narratives about restoring the landscape. As much as the communities found in Nova Scotia's industrial belt are defined by the resources they extract or once extracted, they are also defined by the things left over from this process.

The everyday geography of northern Nova Scotia betrays this complicated relationship with resource extraction and the rest of North American mass culture. The landscape of the region is marked by the things left behind by changes in its economic fortunes: among other things, abandoned industrial sites, closed mines, company houses, towns built for failed industries, old Pepsi signs on dilapidated stores and ball fields, closed call centres and malls, and monuments to those killed in industrial accidents. The physical space of Nova Scotia stands as a constant reminder of the history of the region, but rather than a romantic portrait of a society set apart from the rest of the continent and bound together by a connection to the land, the story is one of a collapsed resource industry, a toxic landscape that seeps into the bodies of the people who live on top of it, and material reminders of the fall of the region's economy in progressive stages.

The Body

The perceived shift from the industrial era to the postindustrial era has a wide range of impacts on the physical environment and on our understanding of it; this is true also of the body. According to received images of Nova Scotia, the industrial era was populated by proud, white, masculine breadwinners, often of Scottish descent, who dragged resources out of the ground and the sea through sheer will and tenacity. The postindustrial era is much different: during this time, we see the demise of the working-class body, a process that is backdropped by anxieties about outmigration, multiculturalism, drug addiction, and atrophy.

Since the turn of the century, images of *white trash* bodies have been prominent in cultural representations of Nova Scotia. The most obvious example, of course, is *Trailer Park Boys*, a popular mockumentary about petty drug dealers who sleep in cars, eat "chicken chips," and steal food out of one another's mouths. Literature and popular culture in postindustrial Nova Scotia are marked by a series of anxieties about the working-class white body. Wyile suggests in *Anne of Tim Hortons* that these images of disorder are a counterpoint to images of the folk described by McKay. While the most commonly known version of the folk paradigm centres on romantic, traditional people removed from the rest of the continent and the idea that "[Atlantic Canada] was essentially innocent of the complications and anxieties of twentieth-century modernity" (McKay 1994, 30), there is also a pejorative version of the folk which encompasses "constructions of the East Coast as Canada's social, economic, and cultural basket case, populated by alcoholic deadbeats, welfare mothers, and rockbound trailer trash" (Wyile 2011, 138).

In the case of postindustrial Nova Scotia, the concept of white trash intersects with ideas about masculinity (this image bumps up against stereotypes about welfare and seasonal work, for example) and about the landscape (instead of the masculine body connected with a bountiful physical environment, the post-working-class body is immersed in refuse and the byproducts of the industrial era). While this transgressive version of white trash culture critiques the emphasis on the romantic folk and on Scottish identity characteristic of the province, it also might constitute an articulation of white innocence in a province sometimes referred to as the "Mississippi of the North." At the same time, white trash images allow authors and cultural producers to explore concepts surrounding class, the family, the body, contagion, and the often-porous boundary between nature and culture (Algeo 2003, Hartigan 2005, Wray 2006, Wray and Newitz 1997).

A NOTE ON GEOGRAPHY

This book focuses primarily on what I call "northern Nova Scotia," the postindustrial belt that stretches from Springhill to Sydney. I occasionally move outside of this geographic area, particularly in chapter 5, but generally stay with representations of communities in which the fall of manufacturing and primary industries has restructured social relations and impacted understandings of race, gender, nature, and the working-class body. Because of this general framework, the book has a number of limitations: my focus on this rural area means I do not fully cover Halifax's vibrant literary and musical scene and my own linguistic competency (or lack thereof) keeps me from dealing with Acadian literature and popular culture.

My attempt to stitch together this cultural region is guided in part by a very specific metaphor that comes up in a number of the texts I have chosen – the description of these communities as "corpses." Consider, for example, Ziv's account of Albion Mines in *Twenty-Six*: "When you stood back from this place you could see the marks, like looking at the rings of a stump: the growth, the stunted growth, the decay, the resuscitation. Albion Mines was not so much a ghost as an exhumed corpse, a half-charred body pulled prematurely from the crematorium" (McKay 2003, 257). Contemporary literature and popular culture often represents communities in northern Nova Scotia in a state more complex than death. Mining and manufacturing companies overexploited their resources and then discarded the communities and their residents; the tourism industry then steps in to reanimate these communities and put them on display in the name of economic diversification.

Using this image as a starting point, this book examines the way in which northern Nova Scotia deals with the byproducts of its past extractive and industrial activities. The state and the corporate community pitch a narrative about the fall of the industrial era and the emergence of a new economy in its wake, but this story is too clean. There are things left over, including communities themselves, the masculine working-class culture, confusion about the relationship between ethnicity and identity, pollution, prescription drug abuse, and the reconstituted version of history presented by the tourism industry.

OUTLINE

The first chapter provides the historical context for the overall argument, examining the way in which twentieth-century authors approach the book's key concepts, including the impact of resource extraction, narratives of masculine sacrifice, the idea of communities bound to the landscape through patterns of work (and the racial politics of such accounts), and the memorialization of the industrial era. I specifically focus on the work of Dawn Fraser, Hugh MacLennan, and Alistair MacLeod, suggesting that an ambivalent response to coal mining and its byproducts has long been a key part of Nova Scotian literature and popular culture. These authors counter romanticized accounts of the industry, calling attention to the exploitation of workers, its environmental impacts, changing patterns of work, and the way in which the tourism industry has attempted to monetize and place on display an a-critical version of the history of resource extraction in the province. The rest of the book focuses on the way in which the literature and popular culture of the twenty-first century – Nova Scotia's so-called "postindustrial" era – responds to and builds on the work of these authors.

In chapter 2, I establish the geographic focus of the book, sketching the framework of postindustrial Nova Scotia as the area serviced by the Miners Memorial Highway from Springhill to the Canso Causeway and the Colliery Route between Sydney and Glace Bay. This chapter focuses on the tension between the official narrative of the industrial history of the province depicted in museums and monuments and the work of Leo McKay, Jonathan Campbell, and Frank Macdonald. Exhibition mines and other heritage spaces focus on nostalgic accounts of the bravery and sacrifice of the men who worked in dangerous extractive and industrial projects and on a clean progression into the world of tourism and the service economy (which, of course, includes such museums). In response, these authors call attention to the presence of the pollution and byproducts of the industrial era in the space of contemporary Nova Scotia.

In spite of the prominent role that representations of masculinity has played in Atlantic Canadian writing and popular culture (think of David Adams Richards, Michael Winter, *Goin' Down the Road*, among others), criticism on this topic is still emerging. Chapter 3 examines the way in which North America's wider "crisis of masculinity" intersects with the specific tensions of the postindustrial space of contemporary Nova Scotia. I focus primarily on three of Lynn Coady's texts ("Play the Monster Blind," *Saints of Big Harbour, The Antagonist*) and on Jason Buxton's *Blackbird*. In Coady's Cape Breton fiction, male characters are either washed-up and pissed-off father figures or impressionable young men who feel pressure to perform masculine activities such as sports and manual labour. Coady's fiction explores the way in which this understanding of masculinity connects with ideas about ethnicity (the school system pushes Acadian characters into dangerous mill work and characters with Scottish names into white collar professions) and how it places both the body and the landscape of the region at risk. *Blackbird* picks up on many of these themes, examining the impact of these pressures on an outsider to a small Nova Scotia town.

Chapter 4 examines the way in which contemporary authors and filmmakers trouble the idea that northern Nova Scotia is a "Scottish" space. Scottish symbols appear throughout the region on road signs, at tourist attractions, and in other public spaces in the province (particularly the stretch between Pictou and Sydney). The work of Ian McKay and others suggests, however, that this conflation of Nova Scotian identity with Scottish ethnicity was the result of a deliberate attempt by the state to exaggerate this feature of the province's heritage and to create a cartoonish version of Scottishness that would appeal to visitors. While earlier writers such as Alistair MacLeod and Sheldon Currie countered this by constructing more "authentic" accounts of the Scottish diaspora in the province, contemporary literature and popular culture in Nova Scotia puts forth a transgressive cultural identity based on images of white trash. While received images of the province accentuate the idea that the industrial era was populated by a resilient, predominantly Scottish culture that dragged resources out of the ground, contemporary literature and popular culture focuses on images of white trash bodies and a largely denatured and overexploited landscape.

The final chapter expands on representations of white trash in contemporary Nova Scotia. Here, I focus on the way in which the white working-class body is understood to be at risk through the rise of prescription drug abuse. Widespread use of oxycontin and other opiates is a common issue in postindustrial communities, as painkillers were often overprescribed to miners; in the postindustrial era, trading these drugs forms part of the shadow economy that emerges in these spaces. In Nova Scotia, prescription drug abuse is often framed as a moral panic and a contagion. News stories and the documentary *Cottonland* (which is the focus of this chapter) maintain that prescription drug abuse is a virus that travelled to Cape Breton from the southern Appalachians and transforms its victims into zombie-like versions of themselves. This chapter reads *Cottonland* against a similar documentary, *Oxyana*, produced in West Virginia, and explores the way in which these cultural texts present the degraded white trash body in what John Hartigan calls "a tense narrative landscape in the zone between Nature and Culture" (Hartigan 2005, 137).

1

The Industrial Era

The coal-mining industry is romanticized in Nova Scotia's literature, popular culture, and historic sites in various ways. Much of this material focuses on the bravery and sacrifice of the men who worked in the mines. The cover of John O'Donnell's 1975 collection of industrial songs and poetry, for instance, advertises its contents as "coal-busting songs, poems and ballad-type stories of adventure which tell of the exciting and often dangerous lives of the men who go down to work in the mines." While the music of artists such as Rita MacNeil and The Men of the Deeps and programs such as *Pit Pony* (1999) provide obvious examples, the romanticization of coal mining is present elsewhere. This appeal to the romance of the coal industry often intersects with ideas about masculinity, as the logic of sacrifice tells us that the men who destroy their bodies or die in the mines do so to provide for their families and that these men are part of an inherently tough culture (Fleras and Dixon 2011, 582). In other words, the toxic and exploitative conditions of work in these spaces are "'read' as a challenge to masculinity, rather than as an expression of the exploitation of capitalist relations of production" (Dunk 2003, 97). The narrative at work here is that for all of its faults, resource extraction provided stability and purpose, and was performed by strong men who are shaped by this experience.

By working from a timeline in which the late 1990s spelled the twilight of the industrial era and resulted in the disintegration of conventional ideas about the masculine body and the environment, this book runs the risk of buying into this narrative of stability and coherence. This story suggests that it was not until the fall of the mines and the rise of the service sector that writers and cultural producers began to express ambivalence about extractive and industrial activities. The reality is, of course, much more complex. Artists have long had trouble reconciling the place of the coal-mining industry in Nova Scotia's cultural discourse: throughout the province's literature and popular culture, coal mining is depicted at once as dangerous, exploitative, dirty, toxic, necessary, a force for prosperity and innovation, and a noble pursuit.

This chapter provides the historical context for the overarching argument I pursue in this book. I suggest that many twentieth-century authors and cultural producers from Nova Scotia establish and often trouble these ideas about extraction and industrial development – ideas to which contemporary literature and popular culture from the province responds. The key concepts I explore in this book – the masculine body, sacrifice, environmental damage and industrial byproducts – come up again and again in the province's twentieth-century literature. This chapter outlines how the poetry of Dawn Fraser approaches labour violence, exploitation, and bodily deprivation in the Cape Breton coalfield and questions the logic of sacrifice that we often attach to working in the mines and going to war. It then explores the way in which later writers, including Hugh MacLennan, Alistair MacLeod, Joan Clark, and Carol Bruneau, explore tensions surrounding tradition and work: on the one hand, mining binds families together, provides an opportunity for generations to learn from one another, and connects communities to the land they occupy, but on the other, characters in these texts often yearn to escape the violence of the mines and experience the ill effects of the industry's boom and bust cycle.

THE POLITICS OF MEMORIALIZATION IN DAWN FRASER'S *ECHOES FROM LABOR'S WARS*

A recurring image in literature set in Nova Scotia's coalfield – for example, Joan Clark's "God's Country" (1994) and Leo McKay's *Twenty-Six* (2003) – is a comparison between small town miners' memorials and the local cenotaph, which is often across the street or adjacent to these sites. These statues form, along with museums, exhibition mines, and other monuments, a memorial complex that communicates particular messages about the region's history of industrial and extractive activities (Frank and Lang 2010; MacKinnon 2013a; MacKinnon 2013b). In *Twenty-Six*, Ziv observes that "the miner's monument over on Foord [had] more names on it than both sides of the war monument put together" (McKay 2003, 17). The connection between the mining industry and war appears in other ways throughout Nova Scotian literature and popular culture: in addition to its role in supporting the war effort, coal mining is portrayed as a kind of battle of attrition, an act of sacrifice, and as a contribution to a wider project of national progress. This section examines the work of early twentieth-century poet Dawn Fraser and the way in which it troubles this narrative of sacrifice. Fraser's experiences in the Cape Breton coalfield and the First World War shaped his poetry. Instead of romanticizing heroic sacrifice, Fraser focuses on the material conditions of the mines and labour violence.

Representations of the coal industry in literature, popular culture, and the media often romanticize coal mining through narratives of sacrifice and war imagery. Although coal mining promised technological advance and progress for much of the nineteenth and twentieth centuries, today it is seen at best as a lost tradition, a dying industry, and a symbol of environmental degradation. At the same time, and perhaps because it is in such heavy decline, coal mining evokes nostalgic feelings and has a strong resonance in North American culture. Consider the last American presidential election, where Donald Trump seized on the romantic and rugged masculinity associated with coal mining, promising to revive the industry and to stop the war on "beautiful, clean coal" (Goodkind 2018). Always the showman, Trump appealed to the traditional, masculine values of coal mining by tapping into the complex relationship between military imagery and coal mining that is often expressed in North American popular culture.

War imagery has a strong connection to the history of coal mining (Andrews 2008). Coal mining, of course, was a key part of war efforts during the twentieth century. Many of the famous labour struggles related to coal mining, including the Battle of Blair Mountain, are framed using war metaphors as well, which is appropriate, considering that in many instances throughout the twentieth century, the state called in the military to places like West Virginia and Cape Breton to quell strikes and get the mines back up and running. It is no surprise, then, that the rich history of language that connects coal mining with war and with national expansion is then taken up by proponents of the coal industry who see themselves in a battle with the environmental movement and with changes in technology. Discourses connecting war and coal mining also portray these activities as acts of heroic sacrifice in which men batter their bodies (in the best-case scenario) or are killed in horrific ways – but always in the name of protecting and advancing the nation, providing for their families, and contributing to a larger goal of progress. The relationship between coal mining and ideas around progress is literal as well as metaphorical: coal companies mapped out and surveyed North America, extended the imperial project and established ownership over the land for the colonizers, provided fuel, and powered the steel industry and the railroad.

As Rebecca Scott makes clear in her work on the Appalachian coalfield, these appeals to sacrifice have broad implications for the people who live and work in these spaces. On the one hand, the logic of sacrifice and the romantic idea of giving one's body provide a framework for exploiting workers through appeals to these noble and macho concepts. Furthermore, the logic of sacrifice provides an easy-to-understand narrative for the state and its memorial complex to lean on in cases where there are disasters or in explaining the environmental degradation and chronic injuries associated with coal mining. Scott argues that the logic of sacrifice tells us that certain spaces are expendable and actually need to be destroyed in the name of extending the national project, that some lives are valued above others within the system of extractive capitalism, and that these events and individuals are remembered in specific ways (Scott 2010). Nowhere is the profound ambivalence toward the extractive gaze (Hodgins and Thompson 2011) and the logic of sacrifice more apparent than in the work of Dawn Fraser, a poet and writer active in industrial Cape Breton in the early twentieth century. Fraser's poetry contests the logic of sacrifice, examines its impact on the masculine body, and highlights the environmental ramifications of the coal-mining industry.

Fraser's work captured the transition from Cape Breton's folk oral tradition to written poetry (Frank and MacGillivray 1992, ix) and gave expression to a burgeoning working-class consciousness in industrial Cape Breton in the 1910s and 1920s, one that was marked by constant fights between labour and the corporations that dominated the Cape Breton coalfield and a bitterness toward the senseless and brutal carnage Fraser witnessed in the First World War. In his 2008 article, "Protest Song and Verse in Cape Breton Island," Richard MacKinnon argues that Fraser's poetry failed to enter the oral tradition of Cape Breton verse in the same way as his contemporaries because it is so controversial and visceral. He suggests, "One possible reason why so few of Fraser's lyrics seem to have entered oral tradition lies in the fact that many are concerned with particularly harsh times and events in the history of the Cape Breton labour movement. There may be a conscious forgetting of these particular kinds of songs and verse. Fraser's verse may be too strong a reminder of a painful period for the songs to enter the lasting oral tradition. The songs composed during labour struggles, strikes, or particularly difficult times may lose their meaning for the people when the events surrounding their composition are long forgotten" (MacKinnon 2008, 43). It is clear that Fraser's ideological position falls far outside the liberal version of Nova Scotia described in Ian McKay's *The Quest of the Folk*. In addition to his interest in strikes and the poverty of the coalfield, Fraser's poetry calls into question many of our ideas about sacrifice and the relationship between coal mining and military imagery.

Fraser's poetry was driven by a commitment to the working class and to exposing the conditions of life in the mines for his fellow residents of industrial Cape Breton. For Fraser, this question often came down to ownership over the land and its resources. Of course, he ignored broader issues surrounding the settler state's claim to the land and focused on the conflict between the workers and the corporations in Cape Breton; as Frank and MacGillivray note, "The theme that the coal resources belonged by the kindness of God and nature to the people of the area was a popular one among the coal miners of the 1920s, and they deplored the existence of larger companies which, by their sheer size and by the weight of their political influence, could assume control of the natural resources and use them for private profit" (Frank and MacGillivray 1992, xx). In poems such as "Cape Breton's Curse, Adieu, Adieu," and "The Parasites," Fraser claimed the space of Cape Breton for the workers he saw struggling to assert rights in a world where coal companies were willing to let families starve. In "Cape Breton's Curse, Adieu, Adieu," the speaker calls the capitalist class "some fat leech" who "Bred famine, riot, murder" in the Cape Breton coalfield. This sense of injustice came not out of a deep reverence for the hard work and sacrifice of the workers but instead from the bitterness he felt toward the ruling class, which in his eyes contributed nothing and simply exploited the hard work of others.

Fraser's work both complements and stands in opposition to the sombre mining and military memorials that dot the main streets of Stellarton and Sydney. These monuments mark the sacrifice of men who died overseas and underground and make the death and destruction inherent in these activities comprehensible. They do so by telling a story of sacrifice at the personal, community, and national levels and by attaching this story to a wider narrative of progress. Fraser's work fills out this story by focusing on the body and making these tragedies less abstract; but it also troubles the narrative of sacrifice by calling attention to the way in which corporate and state power mobilizes this narrative to exploit workers.

In contrast to romantic accounts of the strong and refined masculine body in battle with the coal seam, Fraser's work focuses on the industry's brutal working conditions and the extreme poverty in the coalfield. While his poems do sometimes feature maimings and disfigurings, he is interested in events that are less immediate and less definitive. Instead of sensationalizing and valorizing the wounds that men endure in the mines, or even their dead bodies,

Fraser focuses on chronic pain and injuries, the lack of suitable food and shelter, and the constant threat of work disappearing. A common theme in his poetry is families with no access to food; instead of catastrophic injuries, the subjects of Fraser's poetry suffer long-term and nonromantic plights such as starving to death or seeing their bodies waste away after a lifetime of toiling in the mines. For these people, there is no reward – literal or symbolic – for the sacrifice of working in the mines: they are denied the most basic necessities, spend their lives working in dirty and painful conditions, and at the end, their families treat their deaths as futile disappointments rather than tragedies. Where later authors, such as Leo McKay, and the memorial complex tend to favour tragic moments such as collapses and explosions (which are instantaneous and thus more easily explained), Fraser is drawn to the "slow violence" (Nixon 2011) of the mines and the war.

Consider, for example, Fraser's poem "He Starved, He Starved, I Tell You." Addressing the poem to the owners of the mines, the speaker describes Eddie Crimmins, a worker who travelled to Cape Breton from Newfoundland to work in the Cape Breton coalfield. Instead of calling attention to Eddie's hard work and the nobility of his hardscrabble way of life, the poem highlights the futility of sacrifice: "He had nothing much to ask;/No, not a dream he ever had/That he might work and save —/Was quite content to live and die/And be a working slave" (Fraser 1992, 3). The speaker stresses that there is no reward for the life of hard labour that he describes: Eddie is denied the basic necessities and finds himself starving and wasting away on the "dirty, damned street" (3). The poem directly implicates the exploitative system of extractive capitalism in creating this situation, suggesting that "Capital" has a debt to pay for the conditions of workers like Eddie Crimmins. The speaker observes that the owners of the mines would give food to a dog they saw starving on the street before they would do so for Eddie or any of his fellow workers. The romantic reading of the coal-mining industry – and even later nuanced treatments of it found in MacLeod and MacLennan – tend to shy away from naming capitalism and the exploitation inherent in dragging resources out of the ground as the fundamental problem in industrial Cape Breton. In many of these accounts, the battered and bruised miner's body exists as a kind of memorial to mining's story of sacrifice and progress; for Fraser, though, the question of class is central. The speaker points out that newspapers memorialize the children of lawyers, doctors, and mine owners when they die, but that the workers whose labour makes the society possible are forgotten.

Fraser's comparison between work in the mines and serving in the First World War underscores this point about the futility of sacrifice. "The Widow in the Ward" is the story of a mother who has lost both her sons, one in labour violence in Cape Breton and the other "Somewhere in France" (Fraser 1992, 12). The first son, Harry, was a union organizer who led a strike and ended up "Desperate and starving" (11). Even though the mother says that "There was no real harm in the lad," Harry gets into an altercation with the police who were sent in to bust the strike and shoots an officer. For the mother, this event and the unfolding trial are examples of the structural injustice of the coalfield: the police, the judge, and even his own lawyer conspire to ensure that Harry does not receive a fair trial and is hanged for his actions.

The second half of the poem is about her younger son, Thomas, who dies in an equally unceremonious fashion in the battlefield in Europe. Just as she expresses no pride or nostalgia in her recounting of Harry's death, the mother is cold and despairing when it comes to the soldier's death: "What was the use of trying,/ and fretting about my son?" (Fraser 1992, 12). In both cases, the mother's conclusion is that her sons were deemed expendable by the state. She compares the destructive impact on their bodies that life in the mines and at war took on them. The connection between mining and war is often framed romantically or in macho terms that highlight sacrifice, but Fraser's poetry troubles this idea. In the not so subtly titled "Out of My House. No Child of Mine Will Be a Boy Scout," the speaker recalls his father extinguishing his excitement at the prospect of becoming a scout. His father, a union organizer, tells his son about the Carnegie Steel Works in Homestead, Pennsylvania calling in soldiers to shoot at striking workers in 1882, again providing an alternate reading of the connection between mining and the military.

Echoes from Labor's Wars provides a framework for understanding the complex way in which the state extends, protects, and enforces the extractive gaze. For Fraser, there is nothing romantic about life in the mines or in the communities that rely on them; his poetry implicates mine bosses, the capitalist system, and the state that supports these activities in destroying and discarding the bodies of workers. Fraser suggests that just as these men were deemed expendable by the British Empire in the First World War, they have value within the system of extractive capitalism only if they are taking resources and minerals from the earth. Fraser's poetry provides a way of thinking through the relationship between the miners' memorials and the cenotaphs that dot the main streets of many of the towns in postindustrial Nova Scotia and troubles the state's narrative of sacrifice and progress.

HUGH MACLENNAN

In *Each Man's Son* (1951), MacLennan establishes many of the themes familiar to later fictional accounts of the Nova Scotia coalfield, including the relationship between the masculine body and industrial work, the role of the province's Scottish population in developing and working the mines, the ambivalence characters feel toward life in the mines, and some of the social and environmental problems associated with coal mining in the region. The main plot follows Dr Daniel Ainslie, a talented surgeon who lives in Broughton, a mining community in Cape Breton. Ainslie, a renaissance man who studies Greek in his spare time and feels that his intellectual and surgical gifts are wasted stitching up miners who are injured either in the pit or in fights after work,[1] lives in a tense and childless home with his wife, Margaret. Ainslie takes a shine to a local boy, Alan, whose father is a prizefighter who has travelled to the United States in an ill-advised quest to make his fortune.

The novel engages deeply with the idea that the Cape Breton Scots are rooted to the land and united by an ancient bond. MacLennan touches on this this even in the author's note: "for several generations the Highlanders remained here untouched, long enough for them to transfer to Cape Breton the same passionate loyalty their ancestors had felt for the hills of home. It was long enough for them to love the island as a man loves a woman, unreasonably, for her faults no less than her virtues" (MacLennan 1951, ix). As in Fraser's poetry, the question of ownership over the land in *Each Man's Son* begins and ends with the settler society; in this sense, his work can be seen as extending or authenticating the Scottish community's claim to the land. As I discuss in subsequent chapters, Mi'kmaq characters do appear in some accounts of the coal-mining industry in the region, but by and large, this is a significant blind spot in the region's literature and popular culture. Many of the writers I discuss in this book are dealing with issues related to colonialism – Fraser specifically targets the colonial structure of the British Empire Steel Company (besco) and its treatment of the workers in the Cape Breton coalfield as in thrall to the whims of management, and Leo McKay explores the colonial space of "Albion Mines" in his fiction – but whatever anticolonial analysis one can glean from these works focuses on the relationship between the dominant majority and the British or Canadian governments and avoids questioning the place of these industries in the space of North America to begin with. In this sense, the obsession with working the land and establishing the presence of the Scottish diaspora in this space can be seen as an "authenticating" move on the part of the region's dominant majority.[2] MacLennan's work constructs a sense of environmental determinism that roots the Scots people to the land through mining resources. Coal mining is connected to colonialism in a number of ways: many of the province's communities were established through coal mining, displacing the Mi'kmaq people; the industry played an important role in surveying the region; and as Fraser's poetry documents, the coal-mining industry was an integral part of the British Empire's war efforts.

Each Man's Son explores the idea of a bond between the Cape Breton Scots and the land they occupy in part through its depiction of the region's mining industry. Margaret, Ainslie's wife, observes that "These Gaelic people ... had lived close together in small places for so long they could somehow communicate with each other in a way no one else could fathom" (MacLennan 1951, 36). The narrator focuses on the facial features of the Highlanders – Ainslie notices that Mollie has "a face with small features and a short Celtic nose so straight it was almost Grecian" (134) – and constantly refers to the deep, almost primordial bond that Scots hold between one another and with the land. To the extent that other ideas about race appear in the novel, they are often attached to masculine strength and the body; for example, Downey, the reporter, discusses the boxing prospects of different ethnic groups: "The Scotch never seem to get anywhere in this game. The Irish, the Jews, the Negroes, the Italians – sometimes even the Poles ... Some day I'm going to do a piece about the racial origins of boxers" (95). Elsewhere, the narrator describes Ainslie's colleague Doucette in these terms: "Doucette was a little man with liquid eyes and a dark skin which he attributed to the root-stained water he had drunk as a child. Everyone else called it Indian blood, but not to his face, for Doucette was proud of his French ancestry" (125).

The novel employs these anxieties about race and environmental determinism to establish the idea that the inhabitants of the province's industrial areas are "shaped" by the experience of extracting coal. Just as they are connected to each other through genetics, the characters share a bond with the physical environment, expressed through the act of mining. The opening sequence makes this connection explicit. The first description of the mining town focuses on its identical row houses blending in with the surrounding landscape and women out on their front lawns washing their husbands at the end of the day, providing a vision of an organic community connected to the land through patterns of work developed over time. In describing Alan and Mollie sitting in the cove looking out over the sea, the narrator highlights the way in which they are attuned to the natural environment: "Feeling the air rushing cold out of the sunshine into the shadow, suddenly conscious of the rise of the whole sea, the boy turned to his mother. 'The tide's coming in, isn't it?' He was proud of his knowledge" (MacLennan 1951, 3). Immediately following this description, the narrator calls attention to the way in which the residents of Broughton are impacted by the rhythms of the coal-mining industry: "There was nothing in sight which could send forth such a sound, but the scream of the whistle shot up into the sky and filled it. Birds flew crying out of their nests in the cliff as the noise hung wailing in the air, but neither the boy nor his mother moved. They knew the whistle came from the colliery half a mile inland and they heard it with only part of their senses. It had always marked hours in their lives" (4–5). This passage compares the inhabitants of Broughton to the animals who live in the physical environment surrounding the mine. While the noise of the whistle is jarring for the birds, it has become second nature for Alan and Mollie, integrated into their daily lives. Throughout *Each Man's Son*, the community of Broughton is depicted as connected not just with the surrounding environment but perhaps even more importantly with the mine itself.

At the same time, MacLennan complicates the portrait of a community bound to the earth and connected with one another through mining by focusing on the ambivalent relationship between the inhabitants of Broughton and the town's industry. Many of the characters, including Archie and Daniel, either leave outright or dream constantly of doing so; they specifically cite getting away from the mines as their impetus for getting out of the region. And of course, Ainslie tells himself that he is getting close to Alan in an effort to give him a chance to leave and to avoid a life in the mines. For Archie, this sense of ambivalence flows out of a masculine pride in the virtues of hard work and bravery that develops growing up in industrial Cape Breton and during his time in the mines: "But to the men of Broughton, Archie was a hero. When he gave an exhibition before going away, six thousand Highlanders – men who had been driven from the outdoors into the pits where physical courage had become almost the only virtue they could see clearly and see all the time – paid to watch him fight" (MacLennan 1951, 15). Much of the peripheral action of the novel addresses the physical peril of the coal miners: Ainslie operates on men who are injured in machinery, he recalls the frantic experience of attending to an explosion at one of the pits, and he talks about the chronic physical ailments associated with a life in the mines. One of the main tensions in the novel is the acceptance of this kind of masculine culture of sacrifice on the part of the miners (and to a certain extent Archie) and the rejection of this ethos by Ainslie, who sees a life in the mines as a senseless waste, especially for someone with as much potential as Alan.

The novel also plays a key role in establishing the "Goin' down the Road" narrative that comes to be such an important part of the province's literature and popular culture.[3] In spite of their differences, Ainslie and Archie are united by a desire to be the best in their fields and both feel that they need to escape Cape Breton in order to achieve this: Ainslie goes to Europe and Archie sets off for the United States to test himself against the best in the world. Ainslie speaks directly to this desire to leave and how it relates to the presence of the mines; he tells Dougald, "There's more to Cape Breton than the mines ... They're only a – a corruption," to which Dougald replies, "Yes, there's more here in Cape Breton than that. And each year the best of the island emigrates. We're a dispersed people doomed to fight for lost causes" (MacLennan 1951, 67). In addition to the ambivalent feelings Archie and Ainslie express about mining at a personal level, *Each Man's Son* also provides an early and mild intervention into the environmental fallout of the mining industry. While Fraser's poetry focuses exclusively on the impact of the mining industry on the bodies of the workers, later texts consider more fully the ecological ramifications of the province's reliance on resource extraction. The narrator observes that the seam the men are working is starting to run out and that the towns that surround it are under threat because of this lifestyle and this resource fading away. Ainslie teaches Alan about the environmental issues associated with the mine, warning him not to drink the water from his brook, since "Some chemicals are seeping into it from the mine and it's not fit to drink" (123). *Each Man's Son* embodies the contradictory response to resource extraction that is characteristic of Nova Scotian literature and popular culture: on the one hand, industrial development and work structure community and connect the inhabitants of Cape Breton to the landscape, but on the other it is a destructive force that batters the bodies of workers, traps men in an unwanted lifestyle, and has negative impacts on the natural environment.

ALISTAIR MACLEOD

Alistair MacLeod's fiction provides a bridge between earlier writers such as MacLennan and Fraser, whose world view is so immersed in the experience of coal mining in Nova Scotia, and later writers such as Leo McKay and Lynn Coady, whose characters' relationships with the extractive economy are defined through the memory of industry and the destabilizing and ongoing period of deindustrialization. Much of the criticism on MacLeod's work focuses on his representation of the disintegration of community that comes along with industrialization and deindustrialization and the loss of markers of Gaelic culture that accompany generational change and movement (Berces 1991; Creelman 2003; Guilford 2001; Mason 2013; Williams 2001; Wyile 2011). In "'This inherited life': Alistair MacLeod and the Ends of History" (2000), for example, Andrew Hiscock argues that MacLeod's fiction "gravitates irresistibly towards questions of legitimacy and origination as axes of meaning; and the ensuing textual debates are played out against the backdrop of the dilemmas of the Gaelic diaspora: for example the social ruptures occasioned by the decay of traditional working practices and the resulting migration of labour; the disintegration of ethnic certainties and concepts of sanctity" (Hiscock 2000, 54). MacLeod's fiction depicts the last days of the extractive economy: people still work in mines and many of the men who leave the region do so with skills they have learned on the job in search of similar work elsewhere. MacLeod's work also both expresses and questions romanticized ideas about the relationship between the region's culture and mining. In her 2018 article, "'It seems to bust your balls': Coal Nostalgia, Masculinity, and Energy History in Alistair MacLeod's Short Fiction," Caitlin Charman points out that MacLeod's "nostalgia is filled with ambivalence: although his narrators long for the recent past and cultural heritage of industrial Cape Breton, they are acutely aware that such a past and heritage entailed physical hardships, untimely deaths, and economic difficulties" (Charman 2018, 60). Some of his characters seem to buy into the ideas of having coal in the blood and that the region's culture is at least in part determined by patterns of work and its relationship with the environment, but at the same time many reject this way of thinking outright.

This dichotomy is clearly expressed, for example, in "The Vastness of the Dark" (1971). James's grandfather tells him, "Once you start, it takes a hold of you, once you drink underground water, you will always come back to drink some more. The water gets in your blood. It is in all of our blood. We have been working in the mines here since 1873" (MacLeod 2000, 35). This account of working in the mines and the role of this activity in determining the region's culture is immediately countered by James's recollection of the horrors of working in an illegal bootleg mine with his father, where he was in constant fear of being crushed, where rats were crawling on him, and where he struggled to breathe foul, "powder-heavy air" (35). As he is getting ready to leave, James is unsure which is greater – his fear of working in the mines because of the harsh life that comes with it, or his fear that even that unappealing future is unavailable to him. When he tells his parents and grandparents that he is moving away to Blind River to find work, he is disappointed that they are not more broken up about the prospect of him leaving. His grandmother shows him his father's pay slips, providing a glimpse into the historical geography of mining in North America: he has worked in Harlan, Kentucky; Wilkes-Barre, Pennsylvania; and Butte, Montana, among other places. To James's chagrin, she is actually happy to see him leave, hoping that this will save him from the life his father lived.

"The Return" (1971) also examines this tension. In the iconic scene where the family crosses the Canso Causeway, Angus breathlessly tells Alex, his son, to look at "Cape Breton," insisting that this place has shaped him even though this is his first time visiting since he moved to Montreal. Later, Angus tells his son, "It is not that easy to change what is a part of you" (MacLeod 2000, 92) when his grandfather covers Alex with coal dust at the mine. Alex's grandmother gets into an argument with Angus, claiming that she has lost three sons: "And what is the something you two became?

A lawyer whom we never see and a doctor who committed suicide when he was twenty-seven. Lost to us the both of you. More lost than Andrew who is buried under tons of rock two miles beneath the sea and who never saw a college door" (87). The tension between staying and enduring a gruelling life in Cape Breton and leaving and turning one's back on family is a recurring theme in MacLeod's work.[4] Instead of romanticized accounts of the coal-mining industry, MacLeod's fiction features matter-of-fact renditions of industrial violence unredeemed by participating in activities dear to one's family and culture. Consider, for example, this passage from "The Closing Down of Summer" (1976): "Death in the shafts and in the drifts is always violent and very often the body is so crushed or so blown apart that it can not be reassembled properly for exposure in the coffin. Most of us have accompanied the grisly remains of such bodies trussed up in plastic bags on trains and planes and automobiles, and delivered them up to the local undertaker" (MacLeod 2000, 187). MacLeod's fiction pulls no punches about the violence inherent in industrial activities; even as it laments a dying way of life and constructs a deep sense of dislocation that comes along with restructuring the economy, MacLeod's work refuses the narrative of valorizing masculine sacrifice so often found in accounts of the coal-mining industry.

Throughout MacLeod's short stories and in *No Great Mischief* (1999), there is a constant negotiation between being rooted to a place and being rooted to patterns of work. MacLeod's exploration of dislocation focuses on the loss of these interconnected markers of identity, with the men who travel around the world to mining sites in *No Great Mischief* and "The Closing Down of Summer" being prime examples of characters searching for connection through work in the absence of a sense of place. Jody Mason suggests that "In his 1999 novel *No Great Mischief*, MacLeod traces a genealogy that connects a very old Celtic labour diaspora to the contemporary labour diaspora created by guest worker programs ... *No Great Mischief* is apparently about clan, blood ties, and region, but its complex analogies create a kind of metaphorical family of migrant workers" (Mason 2013, 152). In MacLeod's fiction, dislocation takes many forms: the breakdown of community

1.1 Kate Beaton, "East Coast Literature"

and family that accompanies industrial development; the emergence of families or crews tied together through patterns of work rather than a sense of place; and then the disintegration of precarious and transient forms of work. Far from romanticizing life in the mines and in small, interconnected communities with overbearing families, MacLeod's work explores various connections to place and to the extractive economy, highlighting the way in which it at once provided jobs and stability, built up infrastructure in the region, and linked families and communities together, but also polluted the environment, was the setting for labour violence, and destroyed the bodies of workers.

BODIES AND DEATH ON DISPLAY

One of the key problematics that emerges in the province's literature and popular culture toward the end of the twentieth century is the tension between memorializing workers who die in the mines (or memorializing the industry itself) and the increased emphasis on tourism. Nova Scotia subsidizes a wide range of tourist spaces – including the Bluenose II, the Hector Heritage Quay, Halifax's Historic Properties, and many others – that provide a certain (often a-critical) historical narrative about the province. In the second half of the twentieth century, the province's fiction specifically engages with tensions surrounding the tourism industry's use of industrial heritage. Wider issues around familial and community violence and their relationship with resource extraction emerge, for example, in Sheldon Currie's work. Perhaps most famously, Currie's multigenre *The Glace Bay Miners' Museum* dramatizes the shift from the resource economy to the hospitality economy and explores the logic of subservience and extraction that flows through both. In his 2008 article, "Shoring against Our Ruin: Sheldon Currie, Alistair MacLeod, and the Heritage Preservation Narrative," Thomas Hodd argues that "'Museum' is not only a condemnation of the mining industry's exploitation of a region and its people but also a gloss of an industrial heritage site that, in Currie's opinion, fails to represent the 'authentic' lived experience of the mining community" (Hodd 2008, 195). James Taylor argues that Currie's work, like *Each Man's Son*, examines the destructive impact of the mines on the region's Scottish culture: "The startling contrast between the realistic presentation of the Glace Bay mining world with Margaret's calm final decision to make her own museum out of body parts gives enormous emotional power and significance to the act of dismemberment as a symbol for the death of the Celtic heritage" (Taylor 1996, 149). In examining dislocation in Cape Breton's Scottish community, the Maritime diaspora, and the region's fading working class, these works set the stage for later texts that continue to grapple with the fallout from Nova Scotia's industrial era.

The Glace Bay Miners' Museum focuses heavily on the impact of coal mining on the body; as in Fraser's poetry and much of MacLeod's work, the characters are stripped down and deprived of comfort and dignity after spending their lives in the mines. Margaret recounts her father and brother dying in the pit and talks about her grandfather suffering from black lung – someone has to periodically hit him on the chest to keep him breathing. The story connects this destruction of the body to the disintegration of Gaelic culture; the grandfather cannot speak and finds comfort only in the few pipe songs that Neil plays for him. Currie explores the rise of Nova Scotia's heritage tourism industry and the impact that it has had on industrial development in the region. For MacLeod and Currie, the tourism industry has turned both the region's material history and the bodies of the inhabitants into attractions for visitors. As I discuss in later chapters, this satirical take on the almost cannibalistic version of tourism in the province finds expression in the literature and popular culture appearing in Nova Scotia in the twenty-first century. Currie's work suggests that spaces like the miners' museum fail to account for the complexity of impact of the mining industry – both negative and positive – in industrial Cape Breton and sets the scene for the dark tourist vision of Cape Breton that I suggest emerges in later cultural texts.

Angus MacDougall's "An Underlying Reverence" (1994) also addresses tensions about memorialization. The story is filled with references to the deaths of miners in the pits. Gibbo maps out the exact place where his cousins died in an accident and buys the plot of land above it. As a monument not only to his cousins but to all the men who died in the mines, he travels around Cape Breton and Nova Scotia collecting dirt from the yards of churches to spread above this spot. Thus, environmental determinism becomes not just a way of connecting workers with the land and communities they inhabit but also a strategy for mourning the dead. In *The Glace Bay Miners' Museum* and "An Underlying Reverence," mourning and the display of artifacts come to be key elements of the province's way of life, setting the stage for changes in our understanding of these concepts that accompany the province's perceived shift into the postindustrial era in the decades to follow.

Joan Clark's "God's Country" (1994) also picks up on these questions. Like McKay's *Twenty-Six*, this story draws a comparison between the experience of going to war and the experience of working underground. Just as Currie and MacLeod express discomfort around the establishment of the exhibition mine in Nova Scotia toward the end of the twentieth century, Clark's story also provides a critical take on Nova Scotia's tourism complex. For Clark's narrator, the fading cultural memory of mining allows for this to happen: "she had thought of miners as going off to war, knowing that those men who left their houses every morning tunnelled underneath the ocean in a black trench roofed over by sea bottom. A no-man's land. People seldom spoke of it, of the casualties: the cave-ins, the gassings, the accidents. No one would have toured the pit any more than they would have toured a mine field" (Clark 1994, 73). Emily's experience of the mine tour causes her to think through her ambivalent relationship with her hometown and with the cast of characters she grew up with. Although she feels strange taking a tour of a place that she knows so intimately, she finds that the tour of the coal mine calls attention to the dark history of mining's impact on the environment and on the region's workers: she remembers funerals for miners killed in collapses and the story of eight miners who were trapped underground for six days and miraculously survived the experience. Like *The Glace Bay Miners' Museum*, "God's Country" refuses the conventional narrative of heroism and sacrifice typically found in romanticized accounts of industry in favour of a nuanced exploration of the effects of mining on the body, the landscape, and communities of Cape Breton.

Carol Bruneau's *After the Angel Mill* (1995) also considers the relationship between the masculine body, resource extraction, and memorialization. The collection is propelled by a series of disasters and injuries that take place in Cape Breton's mines and steel mills. In these stories, whole communities experience the effects of industrial accidents: the men seem to be constantly on edge and are bracing themselves for the next collapse or explosion, and the women and children absorb the stress from the high-pressure situations the men experience. Several of the stories are prefaced with descriptions of the gruesome deaths of industrial workers who died in events such as the 1938 collapse of the Princess Colliery in Sydney Mines, lost their legs in accidents, or were killed by strike busters during labour disputes early in the twentieth century.

Throughout the collection, the bodies of workers appear as battered and diseased from the mines and steel mills. Characters describe mangled corpses that draegermen pull out of collapses and the health effects of working every day in the steel mill. The narrator of the title story, for example, says that her husband is in constant pain: "Underneath the skin was burning. Then he started coughing, like the air had gone down the wrong way. Coughed so bad he doubled over and I had to help him inside, where he sat at the table till he caught his breath" (Bruneau 1995, 40). The stories connect the prevalence of death and injury in the mines and mills to a masculine culture that encourages young men to expose themselves to dangerous working conditions. In several stories, teachers tell their students that staying in school is the key to avoiding the dangers their fathers face underground. However, the characters who buy into this view of education are harassed by the other members of the community. For example, in "Any Night of the Week," when Archie decides to leave Blackett for Toronto, he mentions that the other students at school teased him because although his father worked at the mine, he did not work below the surface: "Old man gone fourteen years by then, worked his life away at the pit, above ground, a foreman. Guys at school used to razz me, say he wasn't a real miner like their fathers, crawling around on their hands and knees in the deeps. Everyone ends up six feet under eventually, so why in Christ's name spend your life down there too?" (115). Bruneau emphasizes that the hypermasculine culture surrounding resource extraction in Blackett places men who work in the mines and steel mills at risk and that the community's mining companies benefit from the pressure Archie's friends put on him to work underground with them.

* * *

Literary and popular culture responses to the industrial era have always been complicated and difficult to navigate. The *Quest of the Folk* account tells us that industrialization and urbanization destabilized North American society generally and Nova Scotia specifically and that these processes left people from across the continent alienated and eager to find an antidote in the form of an authentic folk society. But there is a long-standing recognition in Nova Scotia's literature and popular culture that industrial development is a double-edged sword: on the one hand, activities such as mining and other extractive projects provide stability and connect communities to the land, but on the other, throughout the province's literature there is consistent attention to young men and women who feel trapped by life in the mines and the environmental and bodily damage that these activities wreak on the people who are engaged in them. The authors I have discussed in this opening chapter provide the context for understanding this book's argument: they negotiate questions around the relationship between the masculine body and resource extraction, the tension between nostalgia for traditional patterns of work and the destructive impact of those same activities, the complications of memorialization and the shift to the tourist economy, and problems with the logic of sacrifice. They also establish ideas about the relationship between environmental determinism, resource extraction, and the depiction of organic communities bound together by ethnicity and the landscape.

As I discuss in chapter 2, museums and memorials also play an important role in romanticizing the coal-mining industry. The trajectory I've outlined in this chapter goes from ambivalence about the exploitative impact of mining and its impact on the body to worries about the mine shutting down and nostalgia for traditional patterns of work. In the next chapter, I discuss a subsequent shift: contemporary Nova Scotian literature and popular culture is marked by a vague memory of mining and a sense of confusion about the byproducts left behind by the industrial era.

2

Cultures of Extraction in Northern Nova Scotia

Nova Scotia's tourism strategy is organized heavily around car travel. The province's annual *Doers and Dreamers Guide* invites visitors to experience Nova Scotia by driving along a number of themed scenic "routes," each of which highlights a different aspect of its history and landscape: for example, the Evangeline Trail takes visitors through the Annapolis Valley and Acadian communities in the southwest; the Sunrise Trail runs through historic Pictou and the pastoral coastline of the North Shore; and, of course, the dramatic Cabot Trail connects stunning shorelines in Cheticamp and Ingonish with Cape Breton Highlands National Park.

While brochures and commercials focus primarily on these classic drives, the province's industrial heritage is memorialized on some of its utilitarian and less remarkable roads, including the 104 Highway linking Springhill with the Canso Causeway (Miners Memorial Highway) and Highway 28 between New Waterford and Whitney Pier (the Colliery Route). These roads provide the rough geographical framework for this book; they cover most of what I think of as northern Nova Scotia's postindustrial belt. Along the way, visitors encounter miners' monuments, industrial museums, and exhibition mines that gesture to the province's history of environmental exploitation and labour violence and generally speak to the complicated role that resource extraction played and continues to play in Nova Scotia's history and public space (Lemky and Jolliffe 2011).

In this chapter, I discuss several heritage sites in northern Nova Scotia, including the Springhill Mine, the Cape Breton Miners' Museum, and to a lesser extent the Nova Scotia Museum of Industry, paying attention to the way in which they communicate ideas about the province's industrial history. In the second section of the chapter, I examine three novels from this region, Leo McKay's *Twenty-Six* (2003), Jonathan Campbell's *Tarcadia* (2004), and Frank Macdonald's *a possible madness* (2011), all of which focus on the byproducts of the industrial era. These works capture the region's complex relationship with its industrial past and construct a landscape marked by abandoned mines, sinkholes, slag heaps, and polluted sites. While the narrative of the shift from the industrial era to the postindustrial era often rests on a linear progression in which mines and other sites are exploited and then restored, these authors resist this logic and claim the destroyed landscapes as part of the region's cultural identity. They specifically contest the state's narrative of reclamation and progress as expressed in its industrial heritage infrastructure found in this region.

TRAVELS IN NORTHERN NOVA SCOTIA

In the region I'm calling northern Nova Scotia, visitors encounter a very specific narrative of industrial heritage, one that relies on a timeline in which the industrial era once existed but eventually gave way seamlessly to the postindustrial era of call centres and tourist attractions. One of the key strategies for solidifying this narrative is by reconstituting former industrial sites as tourist sites and thus turning tourism and redevelopment into integral parts of the process of reclamation. At first glance, Nova Scotia's seemingly contradictory approach to tourism (simultaneously attracting visitors to beautiful natural scenery and to sites where the natural environment has been destroyed through extractive processes) is an example of what scholars in heritage studies call dissonance (Tunbridge and Ashworth 1996). Miners' museums and other repurposed industrial sites stand in stark contrast to the tourism industry's bread and butter: the unspoiled natural beauty of the landscape and the quaint and hospitable people who live on it. These activities are inextricably linked, though: the tourism industry plays an important role in glossing over the destruction of bodies and nature inherent in the industrial economy.

While tourism garners a significant amount of attention from literary, historical, and cultural studies in Atlantic Canada, most of the work on this topic focuses on the pull of the "folk paradigm" and the region's picturesque scenery (See McKay 1994; Muise 1998; Overton 1996; Wyile 2008). The province's industrial heritage clashes with this version of Nova Scotia; it offers instead a window into the destructive impact of resource extraction on the province's environment and (perhaps inadvertently) calls attention to lingering ecological and health-related problems. In what follows, I suggest that the unique built environments found in exhibition mines and industrial museums in northern Nova Scotia represent examples of thanatourism or dark tourism. Both the Springhill Miners' Museum and the Cape Breton Miners' Museum feature a simulated mine into which visitors descend to learn about mining techniques, the dates of explosions and fires, and the uses of coal.

Like other dark tourist sites, these spaces expose visitors to images of death and suffering and offer an opportunity to memorialize the past and learn about unpleasant events (Dunkley et al. 2011; Edwards and Coit 1996; Stone and Sharpley 2008). They accentuate the mining industry's terrible working conditions and the effects of this work on the bodies of miners and also bring visitors to see the economic and social issues facing postindustrial communities such as Glace Bay. In their 2011 article, "The Polysemy of Punishment: Dark Tourism and Ontario's Penal History Museums," Kevin Walby and Justin Piché argue that dark tourism is often organized around discourses of reform. They suggest that penal museums locate oppression and torture as things that happened in a distant past in an effort to cast contemporary jails in a positive and progressive light. In this way, dark tourist sites exist for the purpose of giving access to unsavoury elements of Canada's past within highly controlled and mediated environments. The miners' museums in northern Nova Scotia employ a similarly strict timeline and narrative of restoration in emphasizing the transition from the industrial era to the postindustrial era and the positive impacts of this shift.

At first glance, these sites seem to complicate the particular tourist gaze that McKay and others identify; ultimately, however, they work to memorialize the region's industrial history in a straightforward and at times romantic way. In his 2015 article "Regenerating Cultural Identity through Industrial Tourism," Robert Summerby-Murray examines the visitor experience at several deindustrialized heritage sites in Atlantic Canada, including the Springhill Mine and the Nova Scotia Museum of Industry. He argues that while these sites seek to create "authentic" representations of the past, they do so within strict boundaries: "This reflects visitors' expectations of the past, founded on images and real examples that are in their collective consciousness. Dirt, noise, environmental pollution are also in this expectation but it is clear that site managers have worked hard to downplay these negative environmental issues or to contain them" (Summerby-Murray 2015, 84). By exposing visitors to the dark elements of the region's industrial past, these museums highlight the human and environmental effects of mining. They also, however, package the experience in an overall narrative of progress and development that reconciles this knowledge with the fact that contemporary society benefits greatly from this industry. The dark edges of these exhibits are softened by references to the bravery of the miners and their participation in the project of constructing Canada, and visitors are placed at a safe distance from the terrible working conditions and destructive after-effects of mining.

In her work on coal-mining heritage sites in West Virginia, Rebecca Scott argues that in the postindustrial era, regions that have been "used up" by mining companies are often transformed into tourist-friendly spaces that market a stripped-down version of the history of resource extraction to visitors. For Scott, marginal regions such as Appalachia and Atlantic Canada are "uncanny" spaces that exist at the periphery of cultural or economic life in North America but also paradoxically represent "real" or "authentic" lifestyles threatened by technology and mass communications

(Scott 2010, 10). Miners' museums in Nova Scotia capture the complex relationship between Atlantic Canada and the rest of the country and present this kind of dark but sanitized version of the region's history of coal mining through guided tours of simulated mines and exhibits.

***

In Springhill, a student guide takes visitors through the mine and talks about the poor working conditions and how both the miners and their families lived in constant fear of explosions and fires. The guide notes the prevalence of diseases such as black lung and the frequency with which miners were injured on the job. In particular, the guide highlights the constant dangers miners faced, including workers losing hands and arms on the coal cart that took them to the face and explosions and collapses that varied in severity. The 1958 Springhill Bump in which seventy-five men were killed and over one hundred were trapped in the mine provides much of the backdrop of the guide's extensive discussion of the dangers and disasters inherent in coal mining in the region.

While the Springhill exhibition mine employs summer students as guides, retired or laid-off miners lead the tours of the Cape Breton Miners' Museum in an effort to provide work to those who lost their jobs when the mines closed and to add a layer of authenticity to the visitor experience. Here, the guide talks firsthand about near-death experiences, awkward methods for going to the bathroom in the mine, and the history of exploitation and labour violence in the Cape Breton coalfield.

In both sites, visitors are required to wear slickers and/or rubber boots as well as hardhats for the journey into the mine. Visitors put these on in change houses, where the guides tell stories about miners jostling for the best shower and playing pranks on one another. In Sydney, signs in the waiting room drive home messages about the dangers of working in the mine; one reads, "Your wife and children expect you home this evening – don't disappoint them. Be careful." Many of the signs in the waiting area emphasize that safety is an individual responsibility, with signs warning miners not to smoke below ground and to leave the rake only when it has come to a complete stop.

2.1 Novelty hard hats, Springhill Miners' Museum

Both tours are designed to expose visitors to the discomfort of working in the mine; the guides unexpectedly cut the lights, temporarily leaving the groups in the pitch dark, and take visitors through small sections of the mine where the ceiling dips below comfortable levels, sometimes as low as three feet in the case of Glace Bay. At the same time, the guides emphasize humour and bravery in their accounts of these unpleasant experiences, which both softens the edges of these stories and plays up the sacrifices made by the workers and these communities.

Both mine shafts are surrounded by a reconstructed version of a quaint mining village. The mining village in Glace Bay is more elaborate and includes a functioning company store, restaurant, and main street. These makeshift villages freeze the history of coal mining in a specific moment, with the guide in Springhill talking about what life might have resembled in the 1920s and technological advances that allowed miners to use kerosene and then battery-powered lamps. The guides emphasize the camaraderie of life in the mines, men making friends with rats and with horses, and also highlight safety advances such as oxygen systems and improved rescue techniques.

The tours and the exhibits in both museums construct a linear timeline which begins with descriptions of the geological history of the region, the usage of coal by the Mi'kmaq, the construction of company towns and infrastructure by colonial companies such as the General Mining Association, and coal's vital role in driving industrialization in North America and the United Kingdom. This timeline ends with technological changes that allowed coal to be extracted in incrementally safer ways until conventional coal mining was eventually replaced by strip mining, and then descriptions of the end of the coal-mining era and the arrival of efficient and flexible industries such as call centres, tourist attractions, and big-box retail stores.

The memorial infrastructure on Stellarton's Foord Street employs the same kind of timeline in its nostalgic reading of the history of coal mining in the area. Foord Street is home to a number of monumental sites, including the public Miners' Memorial I mentioned in the introduction, the Nova Scotia Museum of Industry, and a monument at the national offices of Sobeys. The latter is very explicit about this narrative of progress; the Sobeys Industrial Monument inserts the company and its various enterprises into the industrial heritage of the region. The map of Pictou County on the memorial places Sobeys' distribution centre, the Big-8 factory, and its head office next to shuttered mine sites such as the Allan Shaft and composes a historical timeline in which the closure of mines coincided with the rise of Sobeys as the town's major employer. The inscription on this monument reads, "Today at this historic place, as we move forward, the descendants of bygone workers uphold the enterprising legacy of their forebears in a modern industry that embraces leading technology to prosper and grow." This monument, along with the state's tourism and memorialization complex, constructs a historical narrative in which the service industry's call centres, interpretive displays, hotels, cultural performances, and grocery stores seamlessly replaced resource extraction. Further south on Foord Street, the Nova Scotia Museum of Industry memorializes the Westray disaster and other mine collapses and fires in much the same way, offering interpretive displays called "Coal and Grit," "Blood and Valour," and "The Mining Life."

These museums and monuments tell visitors that while the history of coal mining in the region was a messy affair filled with disasters, injuries, environmental degradation, and labour violence, all of these unpleasant events were necessary sacrifices in the name of the national project and that the region has been reformed as a safe and efficient place to do business. Furthermore, these painful memories offer opportunities to the tourism industry, as dark sites add an element of seriousness and authenticity to the otherwise light and kitschy fare often found in the province's tourist attractions.

In this way, industrial museums embody our own relationship with resource extraction: on the one hand, we are horrified by the human and environmental toll of dragging coal and other minerals from the ground, but on the other, we benefit greatly from these processes and need to find some way of reconciling these two responses. Coal-mining museums in Nova Scotia at once convey enough destruction and discomfort to allow visitors to believe they are participating in an authentic experience and also romanticize these events, make them comprehensible, and place them in an overall narrative of sacrifice and development that views the fall of the industrial era as the first step in a shift to clean and efficient enterprises such as tourism.

LEO MCKAY'S ALBION MINES

In *Anne of Tim Hortons*, Herb Wyile argues that coal mining fits uneasily into Atlantic Canada's folk paradigm. While fishing and farming lend themselves to romantic ideas about connecting with nature, living off the grid, and working hard to earn a meagre living for your family, the coal industry is much more difficult to idealize: the history of coal mining in Atlantic Canada is full of disasters and explosions, acrimonious fights between labour and management, and is capped off by a crippling and ongoing process of deindustrialization in which entire communities have been devastated by pit closures and the retreat of capital. As Wyile demonstrates, contemporary Atlantic Canada is defined in large part by the region's relationship with resource extraction: the offshore oil and gas industry seems to promise a way out of the region's depressed economic conditions and a pool of transient labour from Atlantic Canada drives development in Alberta's oil sands.

McKay's *Twenty-Six*, inspired by the 1992 Westray mine disaster, takes place in a thinly fictionalized version of his (and my) hometown, Stellarton, Nova Scotia – an area that for much of its history was home to several of northern Nova Scotia's key mines, including the Allan, the Acadia, and the McGregor. In *Twenty-Six* and his earlier collection of short stories, *Like This* (1996), McKay calls Stellarton "Albion Mines," the name given to the area by the General Mining Association (gma) in 1827. While most of Stellarton's streets, parks, and neighbourhoods are named after mine managers, seams, and pits, the only place other than McKay's work where this name currently appears is on the province's green signs welcoming visitors to town. In 2006, Nova Scotia's Department of Transportation and Infrastructure Renewal established a policy allowing Gaelic place names to appear on road signs for regions in the province where Gaelic was spoken and also created a handy website for visitors who might not be comfortable with pronunciation to find out more about these names and to have them sounded out. Instead of providing a Gaelic translation of Stellarton, the department translated the original name of the area to Méinnean Na h-Albann, a subtle but significant nod to the area's colonial past, its status as a resource base for the rest of the country, and to the state's push to attract visitors to the area by accentuating its real or imagined Scottish heritage. While it may seem like a relatively small detail, this sign (like McKay's work) disrupts a narrative of progress that the Canadian state looks to construct, one that accentuates Canada's maturation from colony to nation and glosses over inconvenient events like the process of settling the country and industrial accidents.

Westray, which took place in Pictou County and resulted in the death of twenty-six miners, is a key event in this narrative of progress. In addition to *Twenty-Six*, the disaster has inspired a number of documentaries and books, including Paul Cowan's *Westray* (2001), Dean Jobb's *Calculated Risk: Greed, Politics, and the Westray Tragedy* (1994), and Vernon Theriault's *Westray: My*

Journey from Darkness to Light (2019). Westray brought international attention to Canada and to Pictou County and led to a wholesale restructuring of the industrial economy in the region (which was already in decline). By calling his community Albion Mines, McKay suggests that less has changed in the time since the founding of the coalfield in this area than we might like to admit. The novel constructs and mobilizes a "spatial politics of difference" (Scott 2010, 143) that reminds us that the narrative of belonging and sacrifice in the name of progress that nationalism constructs necessarily depends on our ability to selectively forget certain events (Renan 1990, 11).

The name "Albion Mines" appearing on these prominent signs and in McKay's texts also calls attention to connections between what John Urry calls "the tourist gaze" and what we might call "the extractive gaze" (Hodgins and Thompson 2011; Morton 2007; Urry 2002), which refers to industrial society's preference for viewing the environment as something that can be divided up, surveyed, and mined for resources. The push for tourism in places such as Atlantic Canada bolsters the extractive gaze by glossing over the environmental impact of the resource industry, directing our attention away from the history of labour disputes, and refashioning accidents and disasters as heroic moments and instances of sacrifice for a greater good.

Twenty-Six undermines this kind of disaster narrative in part through its distorted temporal structure. McKay pushes the date of the "Eastyard" explosion back to 1988 and constructs a nonlinear time in which the story jumps from year to year and events happen several times from different perspectives. One of the novel's pivotal scenes, Arvel leaving his parents' house for what he ominously calls his "grave," appears several times. The repetition of these moments makes the temporal layout of the novel seem arbitrary and punctuates one of novel's key messages: although the working conditions, disregard for safety, and ultimately the disaster itself seem like events that, in Ziv's words, were characteristic of, say, the 1880s, they all took place in present-day Nova Scotia.

Albion Mines' history as a resource base first for the British Empire and then for Canada has a significant impact on the town's physical geography. Ziv and Arvel grew up in a neighbourhood called the "Red Row," a "half-dozen or so blocks of duplexes built by the Acadia Coal Company in the first decades of the century" (McKay 2003, 5). When Ziv leaves his hometown for university, he is struck by the steady growth he encounters in the town to which he moves, contrasting it with the uneven landscape he left behind: "growth in the towns of Pictou County had come in the waves of the boom-and-bust cycle of capitalism, and each bust had left its scars on the landscape. There were abandoned industrial rail lines here and there, their railbeds gone over to weeds. There were old sheds and warehouses, small factories that had been sitting empty since before Ziv was born. There were factories large enough to house a workforce of thousands, in which mere dozens were now employed" (127–8). The landscape and public space of Pictou County display material indications of the history of the region's industrial era. As industry and capital gradually moved out of the area, the landscape was left with a series of scars and traces that have partially grown over, but are still very much present. In her 2018 article, "Spectres of Pictou County: Regional Hauntings in Leo McKay Jr's *Twenty-Six*," Bethany Daigle suggests that McKay employs Gothic tropes to explore the impact of neoliberal economics on the depressed region of northern Nova Scotia, noting that Ziv and Arvel "exhibit a spectrality that results not from a lack of heritage, or ghosts, but from a lack of visible, obtainable, and potential employment and capital" (Daigle 2018, 170).

The chaos of the explosion and the efforts by draegermen to find the bodies of the missing quickly shifts to hearings about who is responsible for the disaster and debates over how to properly memorialize the dead. Ziv and Arvel recall legendary stories about the violence of coal mining in Albion Mines: they cite off the top of their heads the approximate number of people killed mining coal in the region, they remember that their relatives talked about coal miners using the same hushed tones of respect and fear that they reserved for soldiers in the war (McKay 2003, 252), and the narrator says that Ziv had "grown up with the myth and the lore of the Pictou County coalfield, and that lore was about nothing if it was not about injury, perilous danger, and violent death" (265).

Twenty-Six resists these mythic narratives, in part by dramatizing the debate over what to do with the most distinctive and imposing element of Pictou County's postindustrial landscape: the blue and grey silos of Eastyard, which were visible from virtually anywhere in the county. After being broadcast around the world in the days after the explosion – for example, Meta does a double-take when she sees them on an international news program in Japan – the silos became emblematic of the disaster: "Constructed of ugly concrete and steel, there was nothing remarkable about the look of them at all. This was the same sort of unsightly industrial complex that scarred the landscape in other parts of the county, except that this was new" (McKay 2003, 266). The silos quickly become a constantly visible focal point in the debate over how to acknowledge the disaster.

Several families push to have the silos protected and declared permanent memorials to the dead; however, the rest of the public and the state want them destroyed. Ziv's friend, Jeff Willis, leads the former camp, arguing that in housing the story of the disaster in museums operated by the state, the government is "trying to sweep the history of this event under the rug. And the death of my brother along with it" (McKay 2003, 375). He goes on to say that "my brother is buried at Eastyard Coal. Until his body is recovered, those silos are his gravestones" (375). The narrator says that the silos are visible from the TransCanada highway to people passing through the province, and that they are "unignorable, one of the most visible landmarks in the province. They are a symbol of all that's wrong with Nova Scotia's political and economic life" (375). Ziv decides to join Willis in this fight, stating that "The two pale columns of featureless concrete could not look more like a memorial if they were originally designed that way" (382) and noting that the families of Eastyard are lucky to have such a powerful reminder of what happened embedded in the landscape. The families on this side of the debate argue that the abandoned silos represent a powerful rebuke to the straightforward narrative of the disaster produced by the state's memorial complex (Edensor 2005, 101).

Of course, the real silos were destroyed in 1998 in a very public and ritualized display and the story of Westray was transported across the river to the Nova Scotia Museum of Industry. Steven High argues that the destruction of factories, grain elevators, and mine shafts represents "secular rituals" in which crowds gather, politicians give speeches, and news agencies provide wide coverage of the ceremonial demolishing of these key industrial sites. For High, the demolition of these landmarks announces the end of the industrial era and tells onlookers that the social and economic systems it once sustained are fundamentally changing. This is certainly the case in Pictou County, where the implosion of the Westray towers spelled the end of whatever was left of industrial expansion in the area.

In one of the final scenes of the novel, Ziv stands on Foord Street and looks out toward the East River, where he can see the Red Row, the Museum of Industry, and the silos of Eastyard all at the same time. McKay's novel forces us to see connections between these three elements of Pictou County's landscape, insisting that politicians and corporate interests capitalized on the region's economic conditions and the always-present history of the mining industry to will the mine into existence, and then turned to the commemorative apparatus of the state to make sense of the disaster after the fact.

By presenting a fractured temporal structure, calling Stellarton by the name given to it by the gma (and the department of transportation), and examining the politics of commemoration in Albion Mines, Leo McKay's work calls attention to connections between the extractive gaze and the tourist gaze. The state and corporate interests divert attention away from the impact of coal mining by treating the death and injury of workers in places like Westray as necessary elements of the story of national progress and sacrifice. In the case of Pictou County and many other parts of Atlantic Canada, the tourism industry consolidates and advances this project by disciplining the gaze of outsiders to look only for picturesque or highly mediated landscapes and by latching on to a reading of the industrial heritage of the province that accentuates bravery, sacrifice, antimodern notions of the continuity of work, and the way that industries such as mining connect generations and keep families together (Scott 2010, 101). McKay's novel resists the narrative of progress that exists in museums – the idea that we have learned from the past, that working conditions have gotten better – and calls our nostalgic response to the fall of the industrial economy into question.

TARCADIA

Jonathan Campbell's *Tarcadia* also constructs a landscape marked by the byproducts of the industrial era. Set in the mid-1970s, the novel is about a group of boys who live near the steel plant in Sydney and spend much of their days playing in the area's industrial waste, building a raft out of salvage materials, drawing a map of the tar ponds (Campbell 2004, 100), and sailing in Muggah's Creek.

Like *Twenty-Six*, *Tarcadia* features a dramatic generational shift. Rory, Michael and Sid's father, is a union organizer at the steel plant. The family's dinner table and living room is the site of political discussions and lobbying sessions with politicians. In spite of this, the bleak future of industrial Cape Breton looms over the action of the novel, as characters are preparing for a massive restructuring that seems to be on the horizon. In addition to the tension inherent in this shift and the resulting impact on the boys' prospects, the generational divide also plays out in relation to the family's musical tastes and habits. Rory is delighted that Sid is learning the bagpipes: "The only one in the entire house who liked Sid's music was Rory. He really liked the Irish and Scottish songs Sid was learning. He knew them, that's why" (Campbell 2004, 19). Michael, on the other hand, listens to April Wine and Bachman-Turner Overdrive and resents that his father calls him "Bodach": "Rory always called his boys Bodach. It was a Gaelic word and it meant – I don't know what it meant. Son, I guess. Or boy. Whatever we were to him" (19).

Michael, the narrator, begins the story by abruptly telling the reader that Sid drowned in Sydney Harbour during one of their forays in the raft. His description of the event also calls attention to his unease with his Gaelic heritage: "No one found Sid. He either made it safely to shore, or he was taken right out to sea with the ebb tide and was visiting the Hebrides by the time they even got ready to look for him. In case you didn't know, the Hebrides are a group of islands in the North Atlantic Ocean that we Scots are supposed to be able to behold in our dreams. That's what I've heard, anyway. I don't know. I've never seen them in my dreams" (Campbell 2004, 8). The novel accentuates this sense of alienation: Michael has heard about his Scottish roots and knows enough about them to make some vague observations, but he is ultimately annoyed by the connection. Rory's generation, the one with access to sustainable employment at the mill, is connected with these markers of Scottishness (they play the fiddle, they know traditional songs and laments, and they host ceilidhs), or least assumed markers of Scottishness, much more clearly.

While Michael is disconnected from these received ideas about identity in Cape Breton – Scottish ethnicity and manual labour – he feels an intense identification with the landscape of industrial Sydney, especially the tar ponds, which he can see from his bedroom window. The shunting of the Canadian National Railway trains below his house helps him fall asleep, and he loves the smell of the tar ponds, especially in August when "the sun really brought up the smell of creosote" (Campbell 2004, 206). Michael and his friends view the tar ponds as a kind of refuge: they can go there to get away from their parents and their teachers and to soak in its unique environment: "Sometimes you could smell the good smell of gasoline, like the smell that fills the inside of a car at a service station on a hot summer day. And the smell of oil was a good, strong smell on the tar pond. After a heavy rain there was always a refreshing aroma in the air, a pleasant chemical odour like a bathroom spray or scented chlorine" (206). He goes on to reminisce about the mix of the other smells in the tar pond: sometimes he can smell the dump, and even though the city pumped sewage into the pond steadily, the "water smelled sort of fresh" (207). Elsewhere, Michael compares the hypnotic sound of the sewage coming out of the pipe (while he relaxes nearby smoking cigarettes) with the pastoral setting of a gentle waterfall in the woods: "Listening to the sound of water spilling out of a pipe, and watching it course by rusty old wires and empty buckets and half-submerged rubber tires was very relaxing and restorative. The entire estuary was placid and quiet and still. The tar pond was like one of those Japanese rock gardens where people go to meditate if they are tired" (208). In the same passage, he makes a key connection between the body and the toxic environment of Sydney, comparing the tar ponds to the bodies of the workers at the steel plant: "Like them, the ponds expressed deep physical exhaustion after many years' work" (208). This link between the toxins that seep into the ground and the bodies of the workers and residents of the area comes up a number of times; for example, Michael describes Muggah's Creek as "a little sliver of black cavity that runs between the north end of Sydney and the steel plant" (81).

Michael oscillates between these grown-up and almost poetic descriptions of the tar ponds and very child-like assessments of the pollution and his relationship with it. For example, he says that the causeway that separates the north pond from the south makes "the two ponds [look] like one of those long balloons that was twisted by a knot right in the middle" (Campbell 2004, 28). Michael's nostalgic descriptions of the polluted and abandoned sites of his neighbourhood provide an unexpected response to this kind of environment.

Michael and his friends have almost unfettered access to these sites because the steel plant has discarded them: the wreck of the *Bitiby*, Slag Mountain, and the abandoned rail tracks behind the plant become places where the boys are free from grown-up authority and where they can hide from their parents and teachers: "We found an abandoned stretch of rail track with an abandoned line of train cars on it. There was an engine, a few flat cars, a coal car, and a caboose. The train cars were just sitting there on a track that went nowhere. We stayed there for quite some time ... We could see all around so no fat bastards in over-heated Impalas could sneak up on us ... It was just great" (Campbell 2004, 33). When the boys slide down Slag Mountain, they yell things like "Geronimo," and Michael describes Cosmo as "a California surfer" (35). The absurdity of the boys playing so enthusiastically in this kind of environment is accentuated when they come into contact with adults. One man who sees them playing in the train yards informs them that he is "morally obligated to do something when [he sees] children playing in an environment that is so obviously dangerous" (40), which confuses the boys because they know the train yard so well and never thought of it as dangerous in any way.

Tarcadia directly addresses the role of what Raymond Williams calls "byproducts"– the things left over from industrial and extractive processes. Michael talks often about how the Sydney steel plant makes the best steel in the world, but the most important objects, for him, are those left behind by this activity. He provides a detailed explanation for the process of creating slag and the history of the tar ponds: "The slag is skimmed off and put in twenty-two-ton trucks and dumped on Slag Mountain, which faces the north end ... Anyway, you need coke to make steel. And the first runoff or extract or throwaway from making coke is called coal tar. And this coal tar ran through Coke Oven Brook into a series of sluiceways and a giant reservoir and finally into Muggah's Creek. Over eighty years, the tar fluids had turned the estuary of Muggah's Creek into the tar ponds" (Campbell 2004, 82). The boys are able to build their elaborate raft and travel in the tar ponds with impunity because Slag Mountain blocks peoples' views into the creek. Michael describes the slimy water of the tar ponds, the abandoned ships, and the rusted-out industrial equipment that dots the landscape. He notes that if this material were anywhere else in town, people would protest against it and deem it an "eyesore" (84), but luckily it is set off from the rest of the community, meaning that people by and large did not encounter it. This makes the tar ponds a secret getaway for the boys. Michael points out that the extreme pollution of the tar ponds also makes it an ideal place to play, as the chemicals keep away annoyances such as jellyfish and blackflies.

Just as *Twenty-Six* highlights Ziv's alienation from work in the mines and his immersion instead in the abandoned space and memorial infrastructure left behind by them, *Tarcadia* depicts a world in which Michael and his friends are surrounded with the byproducts of industry. Although earlier literature from Nova Scotia often accentuates the idea that communities are connected by work (techniques are passed down through generations) or by the land (especially by extracting resources from it), characters in the literature and popular culture of the postindustrial era share the experience of watching industry disintegrate and inhabit a landscape marked by its byproducts.

After he and his friends had all fallen into the polluted water of the tar ponds, Michael reports, "we had all come to be baptized as legitimate children of the tar pond, proudly sponsored by our extended family: the coal miners, the steelworkers, the railmen, the deepwater pier workers and the dry dockers" (Campbell 2004, 98). Rory has a similar relationship with the degraded landscape of Sydney. He often expresses his nostalgia for the city's polluted sites in his fights to keep industry alive in the region, telling his co-workers that living next to the byproducts of the steel plant is one of the consequences of steady work. When his father-in-law tells him that it might be better if he and the people he knows simply moved away from the environmental and social problems of Sydney, Rory tells him that "it's always easier to clear than to keep" (118), maintaining that there is value even in a landscape that others might see as destroyed and ugly. Later, Rory opposes efforts to clean up the tar ponds, even after it had been discovered that toxins from the site were leaking into shellfish in the area.

While it is easy to pass Rory off as a reactionary antienvironmentalist, he is another figure that reveals the complexity of northern Nova Scotia's response to the extractive and industrial era. On the one hand, it is difficult to deny that these activities have had disastrous impacts on the physical environment and the health of the people living there, but on the other, Rory's ambivalence comes not only from the fact that these activities sustained employment but also that they created a landscape with which he and his sons identify. Ultimately, his position is that the communities that exist on this landscape are an inconvenience to the logic of extraction (which dictates that people come, take what they can, and move on to the next exploitable space).

A POSSIBLE MADNESS

Frank Macdonald's 2011 novel, *a possible madness*, addresses issues surrounding extraction and reclamation very directly. Macdonald's Shean, a fictional mining town on the west coast of

Cape Breton clearly modelled on Inverness, has seen a sharp economic decline in the fifty years since its underground mine closed. Like McKay's Albion Mines, Shean is home to a generation of residents who are constantly bombarded with reminders of the coal-mining industry even though the pits had been closed for a generation or more: "Shean was built on coal but there hasn't been an ounce of coal mined here since the middle of the last century. Just take a look at the place, a quarter of the houses people live in are company houses built by the original coal company. We have a coal miners museum. We know coal. It's been a long time since we mined coal but it's still in our blood" (Macdonald 2011, 175).

Shean is also is in a semiexaggerated state of postindustrial decay: the narrator describes old abandoned businesses around main street as "gravestones," the local high school has been taken over by a corporate funeral home, and children play on top of large piles of slag next to rats and garbage. After the town undertakes to beautify its main drag by building a Memorial Park and a Cenotaph, a local newspaper writer calls Shean "a well-laid out corpse instead of a clearly decaying one" (Macdonald 2011, 11). The main action of the novel is driven by an intense debate over reclamation and the mining industry's role in transforming Shean. At its heart is a conflict over land ownership in which the province expropriates and plans to remediate the land of a local family, the McArthurs, who had allowed the local mine to dump tailings on their property for decades.

Many residents of Shean are in favour of cleaning up the abandoned industrial site. Characters connect this project with the shift taking place in the region's economy: business leaders tell the town that the future is in tourism and that in order to attract visitors to the area, they will need to rid the landscape of these kinds of eyesores. In contrast, David Cameron, the editor of the local newspaper, is apprehensive about the reclamation project, noting that the slag and byproducts of the mining era constitute a powerful, if nontraditional, marker of identity: "Shean was changing. Some of that change was in the shape of improvements such as the park, and perhaps even the eventual rehabilitation of the mine tailings, but those grey and black tailings, ugly as they must appear to strangers in Shean, had always been so deeply ingrained in the character of the town that David had never seen them as ugly. Shean had never been able to lay claim to being a beautiful town, not from the moment that first mine opened and the smokestacks began belching black smoke and mountains of grey slag and red ash began to take form" (Macdonald 2011, 106–7). Although David recognizes that the rehabilitation of the land where the tailings had been dumped is necessary, he argues that wiping out the scar of industrial development will exact an "emotional price" and sees the byproducts of the industrial era as an important element of the identity of the province that needs to be protected.

The key tension in the novel is the development of these recreational spaces and the rehabilitation of Shean's industrial waste. As in *Twenty-Six* and *Tarcadia*, this process is less clear-cut than one might expect: "The Shean Economic Development Plan argued forcefully for the capping of the mine tailings, proposing a thick carpet of heavy clay be laid over the unsightly and possibly unhealthy site, which would then allow the development committee to pursue plans for a golf course, one unique in Canada and modelled on the Scottish links … Coupled with the thriving Celtic cultural arts that fiddled and sang and danced their way through Shean's summers and falls, the town and surrounding county had a lot to offer" (Macdonald 2011, 44). Here, tourism, defined as a mix of the region's appealing cultural heritage and preserved or rebuilt physical environment, is connected directly with the project of memorializing and cleaning up from the region's industrial past.

As the novel progresses, Cameron learns that this reclamation plan is a front for an outrageous gambit for restarting resource extraction in the area. A company called Resource Reclamation, owned by a mining developer heavily involved in mountain top removal mining in West Virginia, applies for mineral rights for the site under the pretense of extracting energy from the discarded material in the McArthurs' yard. David eventually reveals that this is actually a cover for a sinister plan: Resource Reclamation plans to build a seawall that would drain the harbour, exposing the ocean floor and allowing them to turn it into a giant open-pit mine.

David and his supporters argue that Resource Reclamation is taking advantage of Shean's bleak economic situation to convince local politicians to allow them to test this dangerous form of mining in the area. David rejects the idea that the community and its residents are expendable and that the landscape exists for the express purpose of being exploited. David, the mayor, and other residents of Shean oppose this project in part by unexpectedly calling attention to the importance of the abandoned industrial site to the cultural history of Shean; in this way, they contest the conventional narrative of the tourism industry (the importance of Scottish ethnicity and the pastoral landscape) and instead pin their cultural identity in part to these unsightly materials: "he had always felt that the town made up for in character what it lacked in touristy beauty, and the slag heaps were part of that character the way a scar can sometimes bring a compelling aura to an otherwise plain or unattractive face" (Macdonald 2011, 107). David is ambivalent about these tailings throughout the novel: he believes that cleaning up the site and mitigating its attendant health problems is necessary, but he resents efforts to sanitize the town's history by clearing away the byproducts of its industrial past. Environmental and heritage preservation movements often focus on protecting the integrity of natural or historically significant spaces; in *a possible madness*, however, this impulse is complicated. As much as David and other residents in the town are horrified by the prospect of the ocean floor being strip-mined and the town flooding, they are also reluctant to lose this polluted industrial site, seeing it as a part of the community's cultural identity.

***

Byproducts of the industrial era appear in various forms in the contemporary literature of Nova Scotia's postindustrial belt. Fraser and MacLeod explore the effects of resource extraction on the bodies of workers and the legacy of unionization and labour violence in the formation of the province. Contemporary authors focus less on the process of extraction and more on the fallout from these activities, picking up on Williams's discussion of our often-obscured but important relationship with the byproducts of extractive activities.

As I discussed in the introduction, reclamation is an integral part of the logic of extraction: it attends to the physical remediation of the land, getting things back to where they were before (or even making them better) and to the problems that might arise from the closure of extractive projects. In other words, it wipes away the evidence of what happened in this space. The work of McKay, Campbell, and Macdonald resists this logic, focusing on the ambivalent place byproducts of the extractive era occupy and reminding us of the consequences of these activities.

As Wyile and others note, discourses surrounding the future of resource extraction play an important role in understanding contemporary Atlantic Canada. In addition to the impact of the boom and bust of the Alberta oil sands on the region's economic prospects and demographics, New Brunswick has seen widespread protests led by the Mi'kmaq community over fracking. Recent studies such as Alain Deneault and William Sacher's *Imperial Canada Inc* (2012) and Terry Gibbs and Garry Leech's *The Failure of Global Capitalism: From Cape Breton to Colombia and Beyond* (2009) also document Canada's involvement in facilitating mining and its attendant labour and environmental violence abroad. In the case of northern Nova Scotia, much of the region's tourism and memorial infrastructure pushes a narrative in which the industrial era seamlessly gave way to the service economy and to a campaign to clean up and reclaim the landscape. Authors from Nova Scotia's postindustrial belt construct a region in which the physical and cultural landscape is marked by a series of artifacts left behind by the resource economy: closed mines, shuttered manufacturing plants, monuments to the dead, sinkholes caused by subsidence, strip mines, a seemingly lost and alienated masculine culture, and an a-critical tourism industry that increasingly appropriates the history of the resource economy it replaces. In focusing on these byproducts of the industrial era, these authors complicate narratives of reclamation and establish these destroyed and polluted landscapes as important, if unexpected, markers of identity.

3

Masculine Anxieties in Postindustrial Nova Scotia

From Alistair MacLeod's stoic miners and fishermen, to David Adams Richards's flawed labourers, to Michael Winter's sexually and intellectually frustrated hipsters, to *Trailer Park Boys'* fringe lunatics, much Atlantic Canadian literature and popular culture is preoccupied with constructions of masculinity. Contemporary Nova Scotian literature and popular culture often reflects on the status of masculinity within the system of postindustrial capitalism.

While there is a solid amount of scholarship written on Atlantic Canadian literature and gender, mainly concerning the way in which women writers challenge notions of hegemonic patriarchy in the region (see, among others, Creelman 2003, 173–200; Davies 1991; Fuller 2004; Wyile 2011, 127–34;), critics have paid less attention to constructions of the male body or masculinity.[1] This topic is especially important because it is easy to filter questions about masculinity through a nostalgic understanding of Atlantic Canada and its economic and social conditions. As I discussed in chapter 1, the nostalgic reading of masculinity in the region might view death and injury in mines or industrial projects as a kind of heroic sacrifice.

Much contemporary literature and popular culture from the region undermines this brand of nostalgia. For example, Lynn Coady's fiction consistently points out that many of our foundational ideas about gender – femininity, maternal instinct, the relationship between the body and the natural environment, masculine aggression – are socially constructed and damaging within the insular patriarchal space of the families she writes about and the wider society they inhabit. In Coady's fictional world, institutions such as the church and the family work to uphold the idea that femininity and masculinity are discrete and fixed categories. Many of her characters, however, complicate this: *Strange Heaven*'s Bridget and the unnamed narrator of "Big Dog Rage" and "Run Everyday" display a repressed desire for violence and for access to the masculine world of sport; *Mean Boy*'s Moira is gruff, blunt, aggressive, and possesses "masculine" qualities, a description that runs counter to Jim's portrait of her as a "protean mass of female sensuality" (Coady 2006, 25). Coady's depiction of Bridget being forced to place her baby for adoption and her virtual incarceration in a psychiatric hospital in *Strange Heaven* and Corrine's experience of harassment in *Saints of Big Harbour* are clear examples of her deconstruction of the pressures society places on young women to conform to established ideas about gender.

A case can be made, however, that an even more important aspect of Coady's early fiction is a sustained and wide-ranging exploration of contemporary North America's masculinity crisis and the intense pressures young men face – from their father figures, from the education system, from coaches – to prove themselves as "real men." In this chapter, I focus specifically on three instances where Coady's construction of postindustrial Nova Scotia intersects with her depiction of a crisis of masculinity: "Play the Monster Blind" (2000), *Saints of Big Harbour* (2002), and *The Antagonist* (2011). I also discuss how Jason Buxton's 2012 film *Blackbird* picks up on many of these themes, specifically the homosocial nature of sports, bullying, and fears about the working-class body in postindustrial Nova Scotia. The specific circumstances of Nova Scotia's postindustrial culture intensify some of the anxieties these fictional young men feel about masculinity. These texts represent ideas about the continuity of work, the male as breadwinner, and the experience of dragging resources out of the ground as leftovers from the industrial era. The "crisis of masculinity" these characters experience stems in large part from the alienation they feel from these symbols, all of which are important parts of the province's cultural identity.

COADY AND MASCULINITY

In a 2013 essay in *Eighteen Bridges*, "The Twilight of the Patriarchs: Don't Expect Them to Go Quietly," Coady writes about the often bizarre way in which issues surrounding gender were represented in the 2012 US presidential election, perhaps culminating in Mitt Romney's claim that as governor of Massachusetts, he considered "binders full of women" when appointing members of his cabinet (Cardona 2012). For Coady, this discourse was symptomatic of a wider context in which North America's hegemonic patriarchal culture was in its "death throes" and making "the kind of violent spasms to be expected when the (once) most powerful creatures of the land come to a tail-thrashing demise" (Coady 2013, 9). After experiencing the 2016 presidential election, one in which Republican candidates openly sparred about their penis sizes, and the first years of the Donald Trump presidency, these observations about 2012 seem even more prescient. The 2016 American election cycle revealed deep anxieties about gender, including Trump calling Hillary Clinton a "nasty woman" and stalking behind her during debates, and tense rhetoric about "Bernie Bros" (Wilz 2016). Coady remains skeptical about whether any measurable shift in power is actually taking place; she maintains, however, that even the *belief* that white, middle-class males are losing demographic and/or material advantages has important cultural effects. This essay and her fiction are about the anxieties inherent in contemporary masculine culture and the consequences of this "tail-thrashing."

In Coady's fiction, North America's crisis of masculinity intersects with the fall of heavy industry in Atlantic Canada. In the late 1990s, Coady wrote that her hometown, Port Hawkesbury, was clinging to viability only through subsidizing and enabling the local pulp mill and other forms of "big, nasty, smelly industry" during the last days of northern Nova Scotia's industrial era. The backlash from her middle-aged characters against the perceived fall of masculine culture is often filtered through their relationship with the region's industrial heritage: for them, environmentalists who oppose industrial development are effete and out of touch; they push adolescents into "manly," resource-centric professions;

and the region's sense of tradition is tied up with men performing industrial work.

Coady, in both her nonfiction and fiction writing, seems less concerned with the actual material decline in power for men in the postwar era and more concerned with what Tim Edwards calls the "panic" that accompanies even the mild perception that masculinity is under crisis (Edwards 2006, 6). To the extent that her male characters have lost power or influence, their female counterparts have not realized any significant gains. Rather, the people surrounding her middle-aged male characters are forced to spend more time listening to them reminisce about the real or imagined "old days" in which children (and women) knew their place, and cleaning up after their violent and/or drunken outbursts. Coady's male characters are constantly on edge, constantly anxious, and constantly needing to prove themselves intellectually, morally, or physically. Perhaps most importantly, they devote much of their energy to teaching these masculine values to the young men who surround them. Rather than mending this crisis in masculinity, Coady's male characters feed on it and put it to use as a way to define themselves in the face of the threats they perceive to their way of life. The crisis is integral to their sense of self.

Masculine Anxieties

One of the key developments in gender and sexuality studies over the past two or three decades is increased attention to constructions of masculinity. Scholars from disciplines such as psychology, sociology, and, increasingly, cultural studies explore the ways in which varied forms of masculinity are produced, maintained, represented, and contested. Scholars in the field of masculinity studies have made several observations that are relevant to this chapter: masculinity is a fluid and shifting concept that cannot be assumed as a universal against which femininity is defined (Butler 1990); certain historically and spatially specific forms of masculinity have been damaging to women, men, and the natural environment (Edwards 2006; MacInnes 1998; Wyile 2011); masculinity is often defined as separate from and dominant over nature while femininity is conflated with nature (Norgaard 1999; Sandilands 1997); and spaces such as work and sport provide arenas for disciplining and showcasing the masculine body (Buma 2012; Connell 1995; Messner 1992; Robinson 2000).

In general, most scholars in the field of masculinity studies agree that masculinity is a slippery and contested idea that changes according to social and historical context and is thus very difficult to pin down. In *The End of Masculinity: The Confusion of Sexual Genesis and Sexual Difference in Modern Society* (1998), for example, John MacInnes argues that "masculinity exists only as various ideologies or fantasies about what men *should* be like, which men and women develop to make sense of their lives" (MacInnes 1998, 2). The field of masculinity studies is very much indebted to the work of R.W. Connell, who in *Masculinities* (1995), argues that arenas such as sports and work establish gender difference and often cast a certain kind of male as dominant over women and other men who might be marginalized on the basis of race, sexual orientation, family background, and ability. While conceding that masculinity is a shifting and contradictory category, Connell argues that in certain milieus, specific masculine practices and ideologies become "hegemonic." While it is perhaps easy to recognize that masculinity is a fluid concept, an idealized masculine subject – however geographically, temporally, or socially contingent – is still a powerful marker of identity. Connell goes on to argue that these "localized forms of masculinity" shift over time and even might fade away, creating a crisis of masculinity in certain spaces at certain times. Thus, while it is difficult to think of a general "crisis" in masculinity (because such a universal concept does not exist), "localized" forms of masculinity might fall apart, causing confusion and anxieties in certain spaces (Connell 1995; Edwards 2006).

The "crisis" in masculinity that Coady identifies is a key point in much of the contemporary scholarship in masculinity studies. This crisis is defined in two ways. On the one hand, there is a perception that men are losing demographic power and influence[2] and that North America has been infected with a politically correct culture that targets and constrains white males. On the other, there is a growing realization that discourses that police the way that men "should" act are potentially destructive – to women, children, the environment, and even to men (Lee 2011, 31). Building on Connell's discussion of hegemonic masculinity, several scholars in this field argue that masculine culture, instead of folding in the face of these critiques, has worked to appropriate discourses surrounding crisis. This material suggests that certain types of masculine practices – especially recent cultural phenomena such as Gamergate and the Men's Rights Activist movement – are actually defined by and perhaps even rely on a sense of constant crisis (Edwards 2006, 17).

The political climate of the past two decades has profoundly impacted the representation of this so-called "crisis of masculinity" in popular culture. The aftermath of the 11 September 2001 terrorist attacks inspired a return of the American hero, symbolized most clearly by George W. Bush's crotch-stuffing, threat-making, macho persona and the masculine quest to "smoke out" the terrorists (Bjerre 2012, 242; Jarraway 2012, 50). Literary and pop culture representations of the rise of this masculine culture have been decidedly ambivalent; consider, to name just a few examples, how masculinity is portrayed in *Mad Men*, *The Shield*, *The Sopranos*, and *Breaking Bad* (Bjerre 2012, 241; Chopra-Gant 2012, 124; Falkof 2012, 32).

As Eva Mackey and others have argued, many of Canada's cultural nationalist touchstones, including the landscape, hockey, the northern frontier, and even Canada's relationship with the United States, are highly gendered. Mackey argues that "symbols of nationhood are used flexibly to differentiate and define the boundaries of the imagined nation, often switching between defining 'others' and nature as noble and/or ignoble savages, and the nation as male or female, depending on the needs of nation-building" (Mackey 2000, 125). In their study *Warrior Nation: Rebranding Canada in an Age of Anxiety*, Ian McKay and Jamie Swift suggest that Canada's increasingly militarized culture relies on a sense of ideal masculinity (McKay and Swift 2012, 53). Symbols of Canada's military are also disseminated through highly masculinized images such as sports; consider, for example, the

Ottawa Senators, who in addition to honouring members of the military at every home game, call their fan base the "Sens Army."

Coady filters her presentation of masculinity through these kinds of nationalist markers, focusing heavily on hockey in addition to symbols of masculinity specific to Cape Breton, such as coal mining. Coady's understanding of masculinity is also very much wrapped up in her deconstruction of notions surrounding the pure and picturesque Maritime landscape. Roger Horrocks argues that representations of masculinity in much North American literature and popular culture uphold and celebrate the idea that male culture dominates nature (and women, who are often cast as part of nature). He observes that this is particularly true with respect to the western movie, which "symbolically restores to men something they have lost – not simply being able to live in nature and its beauty, *but their own nature*, their own beauty. The snow-covered hills, the immense plains, the 'pretty country' that men gaze at in wonderment – surely these are symbols of something internal to men, that has been cut out of them ... there is a utopian vision here" (Horrocks 1995, 73).

In Coady's postindustrial Cape Breton, this "utopian vision" is often based on male characters' relationship with resource extraction. In his 2003 study, *It's a Working Man's Town: Male Working-Class Culture*, Thomas Dunk argues that the prominence of resource-based industries in places like Northern Ontario (and, by extension, Cape Breton) has a profound effect on definitions of the ideal masculine body. Since extracting crude materials from the natural environment is perceived to be such an important part of the local economy, the ideal masculine body is one that can participate in this activity and survive in this world. For Dunk, this "reflects the macho culture of the region. Northwestern Ontario is a place of long, empty distances, of big machinery, large trucks, rail cars, and lake ships. These objects provide models and metaphors for the human body. Size and power are important aspects of the ideal body type. ... the ideal man in this world is someone who is physically strong and well coordinated ... who is 'not afraid of work' and doesn't 'take any shit'; who does not complain about physical inconvenience ... there is an echo of the ethos of workmen in the staple economy" (Dunk 2003, 75–6). Dunk goes on to argue that even though machinery and other forms of technology have taken over from the brute strength of the worker in physically harvesting and transporting ore, trees, and even fish, male working-class culture still demands conformity to this body type, as it connects contemporary industrial workers with the "pioneer" culture that preceded them. In large part, it is this conflict that Coady is most interested in addressing: John Sr, Isadore, and Gordon Rankin Sr brand themselves as authentic examples of a lost masculine culture even though John runs a restaurant, Isadore has not worked in years, and Gord owns an ice-cream franchise.

"Play the Monster Blind"

The title story of Coady's first collection of short stories establishes many of the themes surrounding masculinity that she expands on in her later fiction. "Play the Monster Blind" focuses on the observations of Bethany, a young woman who visits Cape Breton with her fiancé to meet his family. The story is divided into vignettes called "Drinking," "Eating," "Swimming," and "Boxing," and the narrator refers to the members of John's family as "the mother," "the father," and "the sister." These labels lend the story an air of detached documentary objectivity and heighten the distance between Bethany and her hosts. This distance is accentuated by Bethany's shocked reaction to the behaviour of John Jr's family and her confused touristic response to the landscape: "They stopped at a lookout point, and Bethany climbed out of the car before the rest. In every direction she turned, she could see nothing but dark fuzzy mountains. The ever-present ocean was nowhere in sight, and it disoriented her. She didn't know if this was beautiful or not." (Coady 2000, 18). Bethany's status as an outsider to the community provides an effective lens through which the text deconstructs ideas about masculinity specific to the setting of postindustrial Cape Breton.

As anyone who knows and loves Coady's Atlantic Canada period can attest, one of the hallmarks of her fiction is the bombastic, overbearing father figure. John Sr does not disappoint. "The father" talks incessantly about his own masculine qualities, his past as a semiprofessional boxer, and his ability to hold liquor. Like his father, John Jr wears clothes appropriate for working in the woods – in Bethany's estimation, "not because it was fashionable, and not fashionably [but because she] imagined they all must dress like that, that it must be a very welcoming place, rustic and simple and safe, just like John himself" (Coady 2000, 4). She reports that he is built from "hard, stubborn fat" (4). John and his siblings struggle with body-image issues: his brother Hugh exclusively wears shirts that trumpet his masculine prowess, his sister Ann has experienced anorexia, and John has a history of jeopardizing his health to achieve an ideal body type: "He told her he used to be fat. He was very sensitive about it. He told her that he had never told that to anyone. In high school he stopped eating and started taking handfuls of vitamins, which made him thin and absent-minded, but his mother stopped buying them and he had no choice but to go back to eating. In university he just gave in to everything and ate and drank until he ballooned. Now he was approximately in the middle, a big man with a thick beard" (4). Coady's fiction often examines the impact of hegemonic masculinity on the body. Her male characters are battered and bruised in fights, in hockey games and boxing matches, and in performing manual labour. The intense expectations their father figures and others place on them to adhere to ideas about the ideal male body also bear down on them. For Coady, there is a particularly destructive irony in this focus on the working-class body and the trappings of this culture. Her characters are almost exclusively alienated from this world even though they obsess over it – like his father, who owns a restaurant, John will never work in the resource sector in spite of the way he dresses and carries himself.

This sense of disconnect between the expectations for the men who grow up in this space and the realities of life within it impact the men in the story in different ways. John Sr comes off as out of touch: his anxieties about masculinity are on clear display, he lacks even basic self-awareness, and he seems to be fighting a losing battle against the world changing around him. By the end of the story, Bethany observes that John Sr resembles the monster from

Frankenstein: "They saw him first, walking with great clomps, his arms stretched out in front of him like Boris Karloff in *Frankenstein* ... the enduring image of Frankenstein ended up being this clomping creature with his arms stuck out in front of him. The problem was that this was what John's father looked like, coming towards them – a frightened, blind monstrosity" (Coady 2000, 25). John Sr's performance of conventional markers of masculinity rings hollow for Bethany; in her estimation, he represents a version of masculine culture that is fading away, even if it is doing so loudly and violently.

The final pages of the story complicate Coady's satirical take on constructions of masculinity. The above description of John Sr makes him seem at least somewhat innocent and pathetic. The story closes with a fight between John and his siblings in which Ann accidentally elbows Bethany. Although Bethany immediately forgives her, she keeps this from John, forcing him to apologize over and over for his family's behaviour. She also pretends to be angry with him for the rest of the night, seemingly in order to further distance him from his family and "[k]eep him up all night with worry, her very need for him in question" (Coady 2000, 28). The story deconstructs received images of the Cape Breton family overseen by a wise and gentle father and the reading of masculine culture that John Sr expounds; however, much like the close of *Strange Heaven* (Creelman 2003, 189; Wyile 2006, 88), the ending of the story muddies the waters, calling attention to Bethany's position as an outsider and John's continued bond with this familial structure.

Saints of Big Harbour

The stakes of Cape Breton's masculine culture become much higher in *Saints of Big Harbour*, Coady's second novel. While John Sr is mostly harmless, *Saints* is much more direct in its exploration of the mechanisms that instill toxic masculine values. In this case, Coady focuses on the home place and the arena of sports (both of which also figure prominently in *The Antagonist*).

In his 2011 article, "'It's no different than anywhere else': Regionalism, Place, and Popular Culture in Lynn Coady's *Saints of Big Harbour*," Douglas Ivison notes that Coady's deconstruction of traditional stereotypes related to Cape Breton is filtered in part through her exploration of masculinity. Ivison focuses specifically on Isadore, who "demonstrates anxieties about his place in the family, the community and society ... and responds to the threats to this identity through his hypermasculine and often excessively violent performance in a desperate attempt to 'stop the world from getting worse'" (Ivison 2011, 117). While Ivison argues that *Saints* is ultimately dislodged from traditional markers of place in Cape Breton, I suggest that the novel deals with aspects of masculinity specific to postindustrial Nova Scotia. Coady depicts a bare-knuckles Cape Breton in which the landscape has been stripped of its natural resources and where men like Isadore fight for position and steal food out of each other's mouths. The Acadian community in which Guy and his friends live is positioned as a feeder for local mills and factories that offer them dangerous and low-paying work while their more affluent friends go off to university.

In *Refereeing Identity: The Cultural Work of Canadian Hockey Novels* (2012), Michael Buma argues that in Canada, hockey, and its representation in literature, performs a key function in terms of regulating and refining masculine identity: "Hockey novels work to arbitrate gender identity in largely the same ways as they do national identity: by signifying within certain pre-existing frameworks of meaning (i.e., the hockey myth) and reinforcing these meanings through ... repetitive rehearsal" (Buma 2012, 145). Buma argues that hockey novels often glorify certain masculine values such as ruggedness and hard work and appeal to an appetite for staged and contained violence that accompanies the late twentieth-century crisis of masculinity (151). Buma mentions *Saints of Big Harbour* in passing, arguing that it offers an alternative reading of the traditional hockey novel, citing in particular Guy's decision to leave his hockey team, much to the chagrin of Isadore. Buma points out that Isadore pushes too hard with Guy and the violence to which he exposes him causes Guy to reject, rather than embrace, the masculine values Isadore wishes to instill. Buma notes that Isadore's attempt to bring Guy into the hypermasculine world of hockey fails and that in rejecting the hockey team, Guy rejects these values. Similarly, in *Canadian Hockey Literature: A Thematic Study* (2010), Jason Blake points out that *Saints* deconstructs the homosocial nature of sports: "Hockey is a man's game in Big Harbour, Nova Scotia, a place where violence makes sense, is endorsed by most, and [is] regularly on display for all to see" (Blake 2010, 105).

As the name of the novel's main character, Guy, suggests, *Saints of Big Harbour* is intimately concerned with male insecurities. Guy's uncle, Isadore, and the rest of the community pressure him to conform to a specific masculine code. The novel's action hinges on Guy's conflicted relationship with his family, especially Isadore, who lives with him and his mother for most of the novel, largely against their wishes. In the absence of Guy's father (who left when his son was a child), Isadore establishes himself as the man of the Boucher household: he orders his sister and his nephew around, lectures Marianne on her parenting techniques, and calls Guy by the diminutive "*mon petit*," often in a "fatherly tone" (Coady 2002, 243). In this way, Isadore appoints himself Guy's father figure, a position the community legitimizes, as evidenced by a family judge calling him a positive influence on Guy and by Constable MacLellan acknowledging him as the "family's voice of authority" (302).

In contrast to the community's positive assessment of Isadore, Guy's uncle is a destructive presence in the Boucher household. Isadore torments Guy, encourages him to attack other boys his age, and throws childhood incidents back in his face in an attempt to embarrass him and maintain emotional power over him. Isadore works tirelessly to bring Guy into line with his own understanding of "traditional" masculinity, which is based primarily on doling out violence, heteronormativity, and the importance of industrial labour.

Spurred on by his anxieties over Guy's manliness, Isadore pushes his nephew into a world of masculine violence, encouraging his penchant for rough play in hockey, teaching him tactics for exacting revenge on his enemies, and showing immense pride in Guy's central role in a brawl that sets off a spate of violent attacks between Big Harbour and a neighbouring community (Coady 2002, 77). When a group of boys from Port Hull assaults Guy and he comes home badly beaten, his mother orders him to quit the hockey team; however, Isadore objects on the grounds that shying away from this kind of violence is a sign of effeminacy: "'Don't be so dumb,' he said. Marianne stared at him. 'He's not a little girl,' he added" (82).

Isadore spends much of the novel establishing his masculine bona fides. He calls himself a "solid man whose life was no easier than anyone else's, yet who always seemed to have a good word and to be concerned with the things that really counted in life. Family, community, and loyalty above all" (Coady 2002, 382). Isadore reminds his friends constantly about his gritty upbringing spent hunting and trapping in the woods with his own father. The narrator reports that Isadore "liked the idea of his own life and world as a fairy tale" (213).

In addition to his anxieties over Guy's masculinity, Isadore often worries that the decline in Cape Breton's industrial economy threatens the region's traditional working-class male culture. Isadore expresses concern that the politically correct modern society in which he lives seeks to quell "authentic" masculinity. The novel focuses heavily on the way in which these masculine ideals perpetuate the exploitative practices of the resource industry. They do so by encouraging men to perform dangerous work for little pay on the basis that to refuse is a sign of weakness. Isadore tells many stories about his exploits in the world of industrial labour – stories that inevitably play up his strength and endurance. He reports that he ended up on "the goddamn disability" as the result of an industrial accident. The accident at once explains why "such a prime physical specimen" (Coady 2002, 223) – whom his friend Alison Mason describes as "the ultimate specimen of manhood," a description that inspires in Isadore "a moment of sheer childlike glee at hearing what he had always believed about himself articulated so unequivocally" (241) – is never seen actually performing manual labour.

Isadore spends much of the novel railing against vague forces in society that threaten this way of life: he brands the environmental movement taking root in Cape Breton as elitist and populated by "crazy people" (Coady 2002, 65). He also questions the manliness of Dan C., Guy's brother-in-law, who had moved to Isle

Madame from Glace Bay to "get away from the mines and the steel plant ... [he had] an uncle who'd been blown up alongside a coke oven, and his grandfather had been crushed underground in the mines" (104).

Saints of Big Harbour also examines the way in which the social construction of masculinity is connected to the social construction of certain aspects of ethnicity. Coady's Big Harbour has a subtle ethnic ranking: characters with Scottish backgrounds like the MacAskills, the Gillis's, and the MacPhedrons occupy positions of relative authority and wealth as politicians or managers at the mill, while Acadian characters Guy, Isadore, and René Cormier live in poverty. Guy is in almost constant fear because his Acadian heritage makes him a target. While Howard and Hugh ostensibly seek out Guy because of the rumour that he has "bothered" Corrine Fortune, they also randomly attack members of the Acadian community: "He's looking in one direction, and violence comes out of the other, asks him where he's from, asks him if he's French, asks, *Are you the little French fuck*? and doesn't wait for an answer" (Coady 2002, 183).

The disparity between the English world of Big Harbour and southeastern Cape Breton's peripheral Acadian communities functions for Coady as a microcosm for Nova Scotia's place within Canada. While Nova Scotia is marginalized by the rest of the country, within the region, Acadians and other disenfranchised groups are subjected to racism and exploited by the white anglophone community. *Saints of Big Harbour* suggests that Nova Scotia's experience of economic downturn pits its residents against one another and inspires a kind of bare-knuckles capitalism in which characters like Guy and John Jr learn from their father figures that it is those who are the most "masculine" and most able to dole out violence who survive. Coady's Acadian characters face the most severe effects of this: Isadore hardens Guy by stealing food from him, tells him that part of being "manly" and heterosexual is extracting resources from the land, and teaches him that he needs to hone his body and be as vicious as possible on the ice and in the boxing ring.

The Antagonist

The Antagonist takes Coady's interest in male anxieties and the "crisis of masculinity" into the digital age. The novel is the story of a forty-year-old teacher named Rank who discovers that his college friend, Adam Grix, has recently published a book that includes intimate details about his life. Horrified by what he sees as a violation and a theft of the most embarrassing and personal aspects of his and his family's background, Rank retaliates by obsessively sending Adam a series of angry Facebook posts. These one-sided posts comprise the narrative, forcing the reader to piece together the story gradually and to constantly question Rank's reliability and his motives.

Much of the story hinges on Rank coming to terms with his masculinity. Rank grew up with an unusually large and muscular body type, leading bullies in his school to refer to him as a "gland-case" and his father to push him as deeply as possible into violent activities, including hockey and fights at the family ice-cream stand. Rank is a study in contrasts: he is big and athletic; he is academically competent and clearly a brilliant writer; he feels constrained by the types of advantages afforded to him by his physical appearance; he is obsessed with genetics and with avoiding turning out like his father; and he is adopted.

Like father figures from Coady's earlier fiction, Gord is petty, aggressive, pious, and overbearing.[3] At 5'5", Gord is much smaller than Rank, who reports that his father has "Small Man Syndrome." Gord takes an immense measure of pride in his son's physical stature, acting "as if he had added my height to his own" (Coady 2011, 9). Gord deploys Rank as a kind of big guy avatar: he starts fights with "punks" who come into his ice cream shop and then has Rank finish the job. He also desperately tries to turn Rank into a bruising hockey player.

Like Coady's earlier fiction, *The Antagonist* explores tensions related to the performance of masculinity in the specific space of postindustrial Cape Breton. Chronically underemployed as a young man, Gord gathers together enough loans to open a fast-food franchise. He opts to buy an ice cream stand, Icy Dream, over a coffee shop, Java Joe's, partially because he cannot imagine people "[sitting] around drinking coffee all day" (Coady 2011, 21) but more significantly because of his belief in the region's working-class masculine code. For him, taking the family out for ice cream is an activity appropriate for the man of the house, while "Coffee was for harried office workers, management types ... Ice cream was of the people, for the people and coffee was ... a kind of businessman's brain-lubricant ... Coffee's not what we're *about* in this here town, insisted Gord" (22). Of course, as Rank explains, the irony here is that Java Joe's, which is clearly modelled on Tim Hortons, does cater to the region's working-class: "A patron doesn't exactly come across managerial timber stacked there in the booths ... You find parkas. Checked shirts and baggy pants – wife-bought. Fake leather shoes. Rubber boots. Work boots. Toques, ball caps. Bloated wallets in permanently deformed back pockets. Squints. Grizzle" (24). Gord's contradictory understanding of working-class masculinity and his attempts to bring his son into some version of it grind on Rank. While the novel is ostensibly about Rank's attempts to come to terms with what Adam has done to him, the anger-filled relationship between Rank and Gord drives much of its action.

Rank tells his friend Adam that interacting with his father gives him an ulcer, that his father berated and was borderline abusive to his mother, and that much of his life has been spent running away from his father's influence. Rank is obsessed with refuting his father's claims of ownership over his body. His rejection of Gord is nuanced: on the one hand, he shuts him out emotionally, but at the same time, he consciously refuses to overpower him physically or beat him at sports. Instead, Rank claims that he would never give his father this kind of satisfaction: "Here's another cliché: every guy whose dad was a prick talks about that moment where he realizes he can take his old man – how empowering it is. But I always knew. I feel like I could've taken him at six if I wanted. I was a thug from the moment I popped from the womb, or rumour has it. Ten pounds, bruiser hands and feet" (Coady 2011, 9). Rank tells Adam that the reason he opted not to "take" Gord is because his father would get too much pleasure out of it: he would brag to his friends and anyone who would listen about how big and tough his son was. Gord's attempts to provoke his son into violence lead to Rank's simmering resentment toward him. In his emails, Rank continually comes back to an incident in which his father set off a fight in the parking lot of the ice cream shop with Mick Croft, leading Rank to punch Croft and knock him out; in his mind, this incident sets off the series of terrible incidents that haunt him.

The novel focuses on the tension between masculinity as a biological given and the idea that certain masculine traits are learned (and thus can be unlearned).[4] Rank's biggest fear is that he has a genetic predisposition that makes him violent. It is significant that Mick taps into this fear by calling Rank a "gland-case." Rank's anxieties about the possibility that he was born with aggressive tendencies come out often in his messages to Adam. He seems to go back and forth on whether this is something hardwired in his brain – in one of the novel's first passages, he calls this "an innate criminality nestled somewhere in [my] genetic soup" (Coady 2011, 11) – or whether it is an unfortunate but unavoidable byproduct of his stature – for example, when describing one of his first fights with Kirsten, Rank says that "the problem with being a man my size is that I can't get away with displays of aggression in mixed company" (30). The key moments of his life – the brain injury he doles out to Croft, his mother's death in a car accident on the way to drop him off at the Youth Detention Centre, and the heart attack Ivor suffers with Rank restraining him – all hinge on the question of whether he is, in his own words, "a contagion ... a destructive force" (113) or whether certain harmful masculine practices are foisted on him because of his size, especially by his father.

That he is Gord's adopted son further complicates this question. Rank is constantly caught between a belief that this kind of behaviour is learned – accentuated by his father's intense efforts to teach him to act violently – and a sense that he is trapped by his genetic makeup. Elsewhere, for example, he reports that when he sees someone small and nerdy like Adam, he is overcome by the desire to "squash faggot" (Coady 2011, 54), which in his eyes is "an instinctive, gorilla sort of thing ... Stamping out the genetic weaklings" (52). Rank states over and over that his aim is to understand and ultimately transcend his supposedly violent nature. His treatment of Adam, however, calls this into question and in fact casts doubt on Rank's version of all of the novel's events. He mentions briefly in his opening missives that Adam (whose side the reader never sees) feels intimidated by the barrage of vaguely threatening Facebook posts and has started keeping a "paper trail" (13) with an eye to possibly initiating legal proceedings (59). Later, Rank describes his own behaviour as "Cyber-stalking" (276) and even goes so far as to apologize to Adam for the creepy and aggressive way he conducts himself over the course of the Facebook conversation.

While Rank goes to great lengths to outline his attempts to reject the patterns of violence that he believes come along with his size and strength, there are several points where he embraces these physical advantages, particularly when it comes to Adam. Rank describes pushing Adam around and writes that he "has insulted and ridden his friend Adam many times in the past – for being pretentious, for being fruity, for being slight of frame, for wearing glasses, for being overly interested in school, for doing poorly with the opposite sex" (Coady 2011, 257). Although Rank obsessively pitches the idea, both to Adam and the reader, that his problems at least in part stem from a mismatch between his physical prowess and if not his gentle nature at least his attempts at cultivating a gentle nature, he revels in the way he towers over Adam.

Rank's anger at Adam stems in large part from his frustration with the specific advantages written communication offers his friend. He lambastes Adam for hiding behind what he calls "the freedom of the page," which for Rank means the ability to observe the people around you and then appropriate them in your writing. For Rank, this is unfair, partially because it allows the writer to steal and distort elements of the lives of the people around them but also because it allows them to do so safely behind their computer screen. Rank tells Adam he is upset because he reduced his life to a series of assumptions and clichés and did not even have the decency to tell him these things "to my face, you know like one man would to another" (Coady 2011, 12). One of the central tensions of the novel comes from the fact that Adam's "freedom of the page" strips Rank of his natural ability to be physically dominant. Rank's aggressive and at times threatening messages to Adam are designed to intimidate him and to restore the power imbalance that Rank is anxious about losing – one that he pretends to resent. In *The Antagonist*, the crisis of masculinity is partially connected to changes in the regional economy – Gord Sr resents the culture of white-collar work that leads to the success of coffee shops in Cape Breton – but even more pointedly to the rise of social media, as Rank resents the fact that a "weakling" like Adam can take advantage of him while hiding behind his publisher and his computer screen.

"YOU CAN CALL ME COLUMBINE ALL YOU WANT": *BLACKBIRD*

Blackbird, Jason Buxton's 2012 film, also deals with anxieties surrounding masculinity and the family. The film is about a sixteen-year-old boy named Sean Randall who lives with his father in Eastport, a small town outside Halifax. Rejected by his mother in favour of her new husband and daughter, Sean dresses like a goth, listens to heavy metal music, and is the target of vicious bullying from members of the hockey team at his school. Sean responds to this situation by filming and writing revenge fantasies that involve shooting up the school and killing the jocks who harass him. The film opens with the police raiding his house and finding a cache of weapons (they're actually his father's rifles) and a video of Sean holding up the guns, saying, "which one of these are going to make me feel like a man today?"

Like Coady's fiction, much of the tension in *Blackbird* comes out of the suffocating experience of living in a small town in postindustrial Nova Scotia and from a sense of alienation from prominent masculine symbols. Sean is immediately marked as an outsider to the supposedly tightknit community; as a result, when this incident takes place, he has nowhere to turn. There is a sharp contrast between Sean and not only the rest of the town but also his working-class father, who dresses in flannel shirts, drinks beer, and watches hockey. His father tries to "repair" Sean by taking him hunting, encouraging him to watch sports, and finding solid manual labour for him at the local rink.

In spite of his father's efforts to bring him into a version of masculine culture acceptable to the community, Sean finds it impossible to fit in. The police use evidence of Sean being bullied by the hockey players as proof that he did intend to go forward with the massacre he fantasized about. They ignore him when he tells them that the people who called him names, pushed him against walls, and told him to go slit his own wrists were the dangerous ones, and they go forward with prosecuting him. The judge in his trial is particularly hard on Sean, telling him that he is out of control, and that he must be removed this tightknit community.

Just as many of Coady's characters struggle with questions about their family history, Sean is obsessed with his genetic makeup and the extent to which his lot in life is determined by biology. He struggles with the idea that there is something innately destructive in his dna: he calls himself "the bad seed" and tells a girl he has a crush on that he was born this way. Later, he tells his father that he would like to get plastic surgery to hide from the people in town – people who, once he is released from prison, vandalize his car and yell at him on the street.

After he is sentenced to a term in the youth correctional facility in Waterville, the issue of determinism comes to a head. The other boys threaten him, take food out of his mouth, beat him up, and call him "Columbine." The toughest and most aggressive boy, Trevor, who is in Waterville for killing a mall Santa who attempted to sexually assault him, tells Sean that he is weak, that he is a faggot, and that he will kill him the first chance he gets. When Sean insists that he was innocent of planning the school massacre, Trevor clumsily but succinctly tells him that he cannot escape who he is. He says, "Columbine don't want to be Columbine no more. Only he is Columbine so they won't let him not be Columbine. Ain't that right, Columbine?"

Blackbird, like other contemporary literature and popular culture from postindustrial Nova Scotia, is ambivalent in its treatment of the family and community. On the one hand, each of these texts depicts a breakdown of traditional notions of community that in received images of Nova Scotia are based on a connection to the land, a continuity of family history, and manual labour. The tension of the film comes in part from what R.M. Vaughan describes as the experience of being constantly reminded of the importance of these symbols at the same time as one has no access to them. Sean is completely alienated from all of this and is marked as an outsider both within Eastport and within his own family.

***

Masculine symbols form a key part of the fading regional identity described by critics of contemporary Atlantic Canadian literature and popular culture. Many images associated with Atlantic Canada are, of course, highly gendered, including the wise fisherman, the hardy and brave miner, the gentle father, and the sharp-tongued storyteller. All of these archetypes rely on a masculine-inflected version of regional culture. The fall of the region's resource economy and the shift toward service-oriented labour similarly impacts representations and understandings of gender. In addition to a situation where working-class men leave the region to find work in Fort McMurray and other resource-rich parts of the world, the memory of the industrial economy plays a key role in the lives of the people left behind. Throughout the literature and popular culture of postindustrial Nova Scotia, characters have a kind of reverence for industrial labour, even though it is unavailable as a viable option for them.

The material I have been discussing in this chapter indicates a shift in Atlantic Canadian literature and popular culture that has taken place over the past three or four decades. Contemporary literature and popular culture often focuses on the destructive aspects of the region's masculine culture, especially in the postindustrial era. While there are many examples of Nova Scotian literature and music commemorating or even celebrating injury and death on the job as a kind of heroic act, Coady and her contemporaries refuse to treat this masculine culture romantically or nostalgically. A romantic reading of Nova Scotia's industrial history accentuates masculine sacrifice and the nationalist vision of expanding the country (especially through coal mining); even though these activities have largely stopped in the postindustrial era, this version of masculinity lingers. The male characters in Coady's fiction and in *Blackbird* are largely alienated from these symbols and ideas.

Adolescent characters in this world struggle to reconcile a series of hypocrisies: their communities have a *memory* of the resource industry and a *memory* of a masculine culture in which fathers and husbands provided for their families through strength and the physical act of dragging resources from the ground. These characters are alienated from the lifestyle represented in these images and memories and confused about what role they should play in their lives.

4

Trash the Kilt: Whiteness in Post-Tartan Nova Scotia

"Poor white trash, what do ya say?"
Joel Plaskett, "Work Out Fine" (2003)

In *Anne of Tim Hortons,* Herb Wyile suggests that contemporary Atlantic Canadian writers express unease about the folk paradigm: "contemporary Atlantic-Canadian literature ... increasingly highlights how misconceptions about the East Coast, especially Folk stereotypes, are fostered and sustained within a thoroughly modern, and increasingly post-modern, commodity culture that has significant political and economic ramifications" (Wyile 2011, 101). The backlash against these stereotypes takes a number of forms, including satirizing the tourist gaze, emphasizing the presence of mass culture in the region, and exploring the impact of globalization and neoliberalism on patterns of work.

It's almost impossible to look at the contemporary literature and popular culture of Atlantic Canada without noticing that this discomfort with the folk paradigm has also inspired cultural products that depict inhabitants of the region as dysfunctional, violent, and obsessed with dated and vulgar examples of North American pop culture – seemingly the opposite of McKay's innocent folk. Contemporary literature and popular culture in Atlantic Canada often features excessive images of white trash bodies. I'm thinking here, of course, of *Trailer Park Boys,* but it doesn't end there: on YouTube, there is Donnie Dunphy, Pogey Beach, and Denim Dugay, and this representation of white trash images is present in much of the region's recent literature. In this chapter, I examine the way in which this emphasis on white trash conveys particular ideas about ethnicity and the fall of the industrial era.

In making the case that Atlantic Canadian writers and filmmakers have largely abandoned the folk paradigm, many critics suggest that the region's literature and popular culture shies away from overt references to "traditional" markers of local identity and embraces global culture (Coady 2003; Hennessy 2015; Marshall 2008; Wyile 2011). Consider, for example, Douglas Ivison's 2011 essay on *Saints of Big Harbour*. In it, he argues that the novel rejects or at least is cautious about stereotypical representations of Cape Breton and strips the region of many of its expected geographical or cultural markers. Crucially, Ivison contends that Coady "[situates] her largely adolescent and postadolescent characters in a world defined by participation in transnational popular culture rather than traditional or folk culture" (Ivison 2011, 110) and goes on to say that "*Saints of Big Harbour* is nearly devoid of references to local or folk culture and traditions. The adolescents of Big Harbour are participants in popular, not folk culture" (114).

I bring this up here because it suggests that the influence of McKay's work is pervasive to the point where the folk paradigm he describes in *The Quest of the Folk* has come to stand as a baseline measure for what counts as local culture. Ivison is sensitive to the ways in which Coady's adolescent characters filter their exposure to North American popular culture through their own specific milieu; however, there is an implication here that in the absence of romantic images of the folk, Coady has stripped away references to Cape Breton altogether – in other words, in this estimation, local culture equals folk culture. Ivison touches briefly on the question of race and ethnicity as it plays out in the novel, noting that *Saints* is driven in part by the conflict between characters who identify as Acadian (including Guy) and characters whose ancestry is Scottish (including Hugh and Howard). As I discussed in the last chapter, this feature of *Saints* provides a glimpse into racial tensions playing out in the space of postindustrial Nova Scotia. For the purposes of this chapter, I suggest that rather than constructing an unmarked regional space – Ivison cites

Marc Augé in calling it a "non-place" – literature and popular culture in postindustrial Nova Scotia often articulate anxieties about whiteness that are specific to the region. In what follows, I examine how this plays out in the television show *Trailer Park Boys*, the film *Poor Boy's Game*, and in the fiction of Sarah Mian and Darren Greer.

To the extent that it is present in these texts, the conflict between folk culture and popular culture is trumped by a shift in how whiteness is constituted in postindustrial Nova Scotia: the rejection of a cultural identity grounded in traditional Gaelic symbols (which are perhaps invented) in favour of white trash symbols.[1] The "fallen" white culture presented in these texts is closely connected to the decline of the industrial era. The bounded and coherent version of Scottish ethnicity described by McKay and others was sustained in part by extractive and industrial activities such as fishing and mining[2] and is connected in this way to the land. As I discussed in chapter 1, this link between Scottish culture and Nova Scotia – in particular its presence in mining communities – comes through in much of the province's literary history. The emphasis on white trash characteristic of Nova Scotian literature and popular culture of the past fifteen years is similarly linked by the closure of mines and fish processing plants, the shadow economy that emerges in their wake, and the overexploited and polluted landscape left behind by the industrial era.

TARTANISM DESPONDENT

In *The Quest of the Folk* (1994), *In the Province of History* (2010), and some of his other writing on Nova Scotia, McKay contends that a major component of the state's mid-twentieth-century push to define the province as stuck in time and romantic – enacted with particular gusto by Premier Angus L. Macdonald – was to ensure that this project established Scottish ethnicity as an anchor for the province's cultural identity. McKay argues that this deliberate strategy obscured the province's history of settlement – in addition to the original Mi'kmaq inhabitants, Nova Scotia was and is home to strong Black Loyalist, Acadian, and Lebanese communities, to name a few – and looked to consolidate the province's image behind romantic and packaged versions of Scottishness (Coleman 2008, 106; McKay 1992). This took several forms: since the middle of the last century, the province famously stationed a bagpiper at the border with New Brunswick welcoming tourists to the province, incorporated Scottish imagery in its provincial flag and coat of arms, and declared May "Gaelic Awareness Month."

McKay notes that in addition to a selective and exclusionary reading of the province's cultural history, the creation of this romantic Scottish character served to downplay the role of Scots in education, mineral exploration, and, crucially, labour organizing in nineteenth- and twentieth-century Nova Scotia (McKay 1992, 32). Scholars building on McKay's work have also called attention to the way in which this project dulled the edges of the province's labour history. In a 2015 article, J.I. Little detects this link between Nova Scotia (particularly Cape Breton) and romantic elements of Scottishness in travel literature and tourist brochures dating back to the nineteenth century. This material emphasized the pleasing traditional way of life of the Cape Breton Scots and oscillated between positive and negative cultural stereotypes – including the idea that they were, for example, at once thrifty, industrious, unruly, and unintelligent (Little 2015, 23) – and almost completely ignored the island's coal strikes and other moments of labour unrest during this time period.

In "The Canso Causeway: Tartan Tourism, Industrial Development, and the Promise of Progress for Cape Breton" (2008), Meaghan Beaton and Del Muise connect this campaign to the development of the Canso Causeway in the middle of the twentieth century. While this project was ostensibly designed to support the flagging coal and steel industry, the construction of the causeway furthered Nova Scotia's tourism strategy, one based largely on emphasizing its Scottish roots and the idea that the province is inherently different from the rest of the continent. Opening up Cape Breton to tourism kicked this narrative into high gear: "It was convenient that the island, much like Scotland, could be divided into a 'Lowland' industrial core, with the ravages of industrialization, class conflict, and the curse of urbanization, and a more pristine 'Highland' area consecrated with a national park and surrounded by the rural remnants of a Scottish diaspora, which had populated the area earlier in the 19th century" (Beaton and Muise 2008, 56). In addition to its influence over the symbolic culture and history of the province, the creation of this Scottish identity also had an impact on the built heritage and landscape of Nova Scotia. Amy Clarke notes that while the "elevation and promotion of the Scottish identity in Nova Scotia in the twentieth century was aided by the survival of the Gaelic language and intangible cultural traditions of the diaspora, and these factors provided a layer of authenticity to what was otherwise a rather manufactured identity narrative" (Clarke 2014, 43), Scottish identity also received material backing through the development or preservation of significant sites such as the Hector Heritage Quay in Pictou and the Glenora Distillery complex (46).

This is also true of the aptly named Cape Breton Highlands National Park. McKay, Alan McEachern, and Catriona Sandilands suggest that the decision to expropriate land from the Acadian community at Cap Rouge and to draw the boundaries of the park around the Scottish community of Pleasant Bay (Sandilands 2011, 64) came down in part to the fact that the latter fit into a plan for attracting tourists interested in Scottishness hatched by park planners and Macdonald himself. Sandilands argues, "To put it rather baldly, the 'picturesque' of the Cape Breton Highlands was contingent on its resemblance to a romantic anti-modern view of the Scottish Highlands; Gaelic-speaking (or at least Scots-named) settlers with established farms that evoked nostalgic images of Scotland were at least somewhat congruent with this view, whereas co-existing French-speaking ones with large families, community fishing operations, and a cannery were not" (Sandilands 2011, 68). As Sandilands points out, the decision to clear away an Acadian community in favour of a Scottish one speaks to shifting understandings of whiteness in the context of Nova Scotia. Although Scots and other Gaelic people have not always been considered "white" in North America's ethnic rankings (Jacobson 1998, 70), in this case they were afforded higher standing than Acadians (and of course the Mi'kmaq, who were out of the equation completely). Sandilands and McKay suggest that this kind of racial categorization and the resulting push to preserve rural Scottish communities stemmed from fears about the "dilution" of Scottish stock in the urban industrial parts of the province, voiced most clearly by Dorothy Duncan in *Bluenose: A Portrait of Nova Scotia* in 1942 (Sandilands 2011, 70; McKay 1992, 25).

All of this to say that the twentieth century saw the imposition of a narrowly defined version of whiteness anchored by Scottish cultural symbols in the public space and intangible culture of Nova Scotia. As you might expect, McKay points to several problems with this. In addition to "simplifying" the region's ethnic heritage and making a tourist spectacle out of the Scottish people who did live in the province, this romantic reading of "tartanism" in Nova Scotia served a political function: "A wide range of ideologies drew upon Scottish history, but it was most commonly used to support a conservative argument. Thrifty, independent, self-reliant; pious, mystical, religious; proud, virile, anti-paternalist; democratic, educated, tolerant: in brief, the Scot was the true liberal individual" (McKay 1992, 42). McKay argues that this is particularly the case in northern Nova Scotia, a region whose history of industrial development, and, more importantly, union organizing, came to be associated with an a-political and subservient reading of Highland culture.

I would argue that writers and cultural producers have responded to the prominence of essentialized images of Scottishness in Nova Scotia in two ways: first, by countering the tourism industry's commodified version of the tartan paradigm with more "authentic" accounts of Scottish culture; and second, by exploring articulations of ethnicity that are unmoored from these symbols. This chapter focuses on the second approach, but the first is worth discussing briefly. While the cartoonish version of Nova Scotia's tartan paradigm obviously alienates residents of the province who identify with other ethnic groups, it also annoys cultural producers of Scottish descent, who bristle at its inauthenticity and respond to it with detailed and rich depictions of Scottish communities in northern Nova Scotia.

As I discussed in chapter 1, literary representations of the Scottish diaspora in Nova Scotia often focus on kinship and a connection to the land.[3] Cynthia Sugars argues, for example, that MacLeod's work is obsessed with "the paradox of origins" (Sugars 2008, 138); she goes on to claim that "In the Canadian 'settler' context, this paradox of origins is highlighted in what appears to be an increasingly urgent drive for genealogy in contemporary Canadian personal and cultural narratives" (147). In the case of *No Great Mischief* (1999), MacLeod fuses family history and Canadian history, focusing heavily on the origins of the *clann Chalum Ruaidh* and the way in which the genealogical line of the family is threatened by the destruction of community and tradition that is at the core of his fictional vision. MacLeod focuses on genetic markers – the family has a preponderance of twins and red hair, for example – and on "intimate discussions about origins and ancestry" (Sugars 2008, 146).

In his 2008 article, "Shoring against Our Ruin: Sheldon Currie, Alistair MacLeod, and the Heritage Preservation Narrative," Thomas Hodd also highlights this aspect of MacLeod's and Currie's work, noting that "Atlantic Canada is known for its strong identification with its European heritage, and its celebration of cultural traditions that are deeply rooted in the history of the region and its communities. Whether Irish or Scottish, Acadian or Loyalist, such ethnic groups find their voices through the countless festivals, historical re-enactments, and crafted images that are produced each year for visitors and locals alike" (Hodd 2008, 191). Hodd argues that the history of underdevelopment in the region has led the state and corporate interests to invest heavily in an exclusionary and perhaps inauthentic version of the region's ethnicity, something that MacLeod and Currie contest through "their frustration over an exploitative industry that threatens to erase authentic heritage traditions from the region" (191).

Many cultural producers in postindustrial Nova Scotia shy away from the approach identified by Hodd and instead construct an ambivalent version of regional identity based on images of white trash. They at once satirize the province's "official culture" and advance a degraded representation of broadly defined whiteness bolstered by an intense preoccupation with the denatured physical landscape and anxieties about bloodlines at the level of both community and family.

WHITE TRASH

The label white trash is complex, especially as it relates to contemporary Atlantic Canadian culture. While it is often associated with racial insults, the degradation of marginal cultures, and a kind of internal colonialism in which northern, urban parts of the US looked down on the backward south, the term white trash today is also linked with the resurgence of a broadly defined rural culture and even a backlash against liberal multiculturalism (Algeo 2003; O'Connell 2010; Sweeney 2001; Wray 2006). John Hartigan, for example, argues that "Quite rapidly, white trash is passing from an unambiguously derogatory label to a transgressive sign under which certain whites claim a public speaking position" (Hartigan 2005, 110). Matt Wray's 2006 book *Not Quite White: White Trash and the Boundaries of Whiteness* also suggests that the term has come to be reclaimed as a symbol of a marginal and transgressive identity. For him, this is possible because the term plays on the tension between the positive label "white" and the derogatory label "trash": it makes us rethink concepts like clean/dirty, sacred/profane, and progressive/regressive.

In the case of postindustrial Nova Scotia, the rejection of folk stereotypes and the coherent and exaggerated version of Scottish culture they supported has in part led cultural producers to turn to this "transgressive" articulation of white trash culture. The best example is obviously *Trailer Park Boys (tpb)* (Byers 2011; Hughes-Fuller 2009). The show's mockumentary presentation of the drug and crime-fueled exploits of Ricky, Julian, and Bubbles in the garbage-strewn space of suburban Halifax represents an excessive depiction of white trash stereotypes. At first glance, *Trailer Park Boys* seems like a radical departure from Wyile and McKay's concept of the folk paradigm: its characters live in a polluted and denatured world that has no meaningful resemblance to the tourism brochure version of Nova Scotia; Ricky and his friends come from very unconventional family situations; the pastoral folk that McKay describes are replaced by violent and inept criminals and scam artists; and markers of Scottishness are replaced by a vaguely defined white trash community (Hughes-Fuller 2009; DeFino 2009; McCullough 2009; Twohig and Howell 2009).

In what follows, I examine the way in which post-tartan anxieties about race, the landscape, and family appear in *tpb* and other contemporary Nova Scotian texts, including Sarah Mian's *When the Saints* (2015) and Darren Greer's *Just beneath My Skin* (2014). These works present postindustrial Nova Scotia as a place where tradition and a deep connection with the land characteristic of MacLeod and others is completely absent. At the same time, they combine these "transgressive" representations of the region and the landscape with nostalgic tropes about the continuity of family. I examine the way in which these texts express anxieties about family and community and the denatured landscape marked by garbage and pollution left behind from the industrial era.

Trailer Park Boys

Trailer Park Boys, a mockumentary that aired from 2001 to 2007 on Showcase and reappeared on Netflix in 2014, derives most of its humour from white trash stereotypes, including sexual deviance, feuds that span generations, extreme poverty, gun violence, drug abuse, and the experience of living in filthy conditions. In spite of this, the show's presentation of violence, abject bodies, and trash-strewn streets is always filtered through a dedication to nostalgic ideas surrounding the family and community. In *Shooting from the East: Filmmaking on the Canadian Atlantic* (2015), Darrell Varga argues that *Trailer Park Boys* "tends, for all its surface counterculturalism, to emphasize the maintenance of family and community in a way that tends to blunt the show's critical impulse" (Varga 2015, 283). Characters in *Trailer Park Boys* live in a marginal space outside the bounds of the law; they subsist on a barter system; Ricky and Julian's schemes are always harmless; and the entire park functions as an extended family that looks out for one another.

One of the key characteristics of contemporary Atlantic Canadian cultural production is an ironic and subversive evaluation of the service industry (Workman 2003; Wyile 2011). Contemporary Atlantic Canadian plays and novels feature characters who work in call centres, grocery stores, and other low-paid, flexible environments. In *Trailer Park Boys*, characters live on the fringes of the service industry and rely on the byproducts of the consumer economy: the park is covered in garbage and debris, and characters make money by repurposing goods they either find or steal. *Trailer Park Boys* depicts a used-up and marginal world: the landscape is denatured, treeless, stripped away, and covered in gravel and mud.

Trailer Park Boys expresses a sense of alienation from both the region's industrial heritage and North American consumer culture through its preoccupation with images of trash and leftover elements of that culture. The landscape of the show is littered with piles of garbage, which characters often throw at one another during disputes and even use to staunch wounds after fights instead of going to the hospital. A common problem in the park is the "bottle kids" who throw glass bottles at cars as they drive by. Characters walk through trash as they move around the park, abandoned cars leech oil and chemicals into the ground, Ricky picks up cigarette butts from the ground, and at one point, the city dumps a mountain of garbage on Lahey's trailer. In sharp contrast with the lullaby-like theme music that plays over the opening credits, the show often opens with shots of the park covered in trash.

Bubbles is a clear example of a character who relies on the detritus of the world outside the park to survive. He lives in a small shed with his cats and makes money by salvaging grocery carts from nearby ravines and lakes, fixing them and selling them back to the local Sobeys. Bubbles lives on the edges of Nova Scotia's expanding service economy: he lacks the skills and education to work directly in this industry and instead provides informal services to the grocery stores and makes a living from the scraps they discard. When the shopping mall attempts to prevent Bubbles from doing this, they create a new service/security position (ironically staffed by Ricky) devoted to stopping him ("What the Fuck

Happened to Our Trailer Park," 2002). In the Netflix seasons, Bubbles develops a business on the fringes of the tourist economy, a "Shed and Breakfast" business designed to appeal to people who travel with cats.

Similarly, Ricky lives for most of the series in a dirty car (called the shitmobile), cooks on his engine, and eats food that others throw away. A recurrent image is Ricky waking up in the morning, seeing that his car is covered in trash, and clearing it off with his hockey stick. As the show progresses, he eventually begins sleeping in a sewer pipe. Lucy's friend, Sarah, often tells the camera crew that Ricky smells like garbage and attracts bees. The park runs on a kind of salvage economy: Phil Collins sells mackerel illegally, Ray supplements his income through selling scrap metal, Cory and Trevor siphon gas from cars, and characters finance their drug businesses by selling car stereos. The show's focus on trash intensifies in season 6 (2006), when Ricky opens a business that mainly consists of forcing Cory and Trevor to steal patio furniture from backyards in upscale neighbourhoods and bring them to the curb. Once they are at the curb, Ricky declares these items to be garbage and puts them up for sale in his junkyard ("The Cheeseburger Picnic," 2006)

In season 6, Lahey evicts Ray, Ricky's father, from his trailer and Ray moves into the nearby dump. This takes place at a moment when Lahey and Randy are in the process of "beautifying" the park and trying to rid it of Ricky, Ray, and the trash they constantly throw around.[4] The show peppers Ray's expulsion from the park with exaggerated references to his lack of status: Ray tells Ricky that he has $23.00, causing Ricky to exclaim, "Where did you get that kind of money?" and when Randy removes him from the park, Ray accuses him of "climbing the social ladder." Significantly, when Ray tells Ricky that he has moved, he mentions that he has found a new place that is cheap and "close to nature," a statement he makes as the camera pans out to reveal that he is living in the dump ("The Way of the Road," 2006). As the season moves along, Ray's situation becomes more and more dire, as Bubbles worries about seagulls defecating on him and bugs biting him as he sleeps, and garbage-men unknowingly cover him with bags of trash.

While *Trailer Park Boys* depicts a dysfunctional community marked by trash, violence, profanity, and bodily fluids, the program is ultimately nostalgic when it comes to ideas about family and community. Ricky talks often about getting a "family man job" so that he can live with Lucy and Trinity, and in season 6, he tells residents of the park that Randy has impregnated Lucy with "his" baby. When Trinity gets together with Jacob in season 8, Ricky tells Julian in frustration that he is now related to Jacob, and when Julian disputes that, Ricky admits, "I don't know how any of this shit works." He spends much of seasons 8 and 9 trying to find suitable accommodations for "his family," Lucy, Trinity, Jacob, and the baby (called "Ray," even though his birth certificate indicates that his name is "The Motel") so that they can all live together.

Ricky's conservative appeal to the idea of the nuclear family extends to the entire park, as he and others employ a muddled sense of genetic inheritance to define Sunnyvale as an organic and unified community. There are subtle hints that Julian is actually Trinity's father; Sarah ends up dating both Cory and Trevor; Barb, Randy, and Lahey live together as a family at various points; and Ricky's confusing contestation of Lucy's baby in season 7 parallels a situation that emerges at the same time in which J-Roc and Tyrone sleep with two friends, both of whom get pregnant, and decide to raise the two babies as a joint effort (in "The Mustard Tiger," 2007). On the surface, the show's presentation of the family seems to deconstruct and problematize the idea of the organic Maritime family present in earlier cultural products (Creelman 2003; Davies 1991; Fuller 2004); however, at its core, *Trailer Park Boys* is nostalgic and sentimental in its construction of family and community relationships.

The show also establishes a complex and ambivalent racial hierarchy in which white residents of the park can appropriate elements of African Nova Scotian identity, and where most of its inhabitants belong to a reconstructed version of white trash culture that sets itself in opposition not only to racialized members of the community but also to the rest of Nova Scotian society. In a very limited way, issues surrounding African–Nova Scotian identity come up in *Trailer Park Boys*, generally filtered through its presentation of J-Roc, a local rapper, and his friends. J-Roc is an exaggerated version of white North America's appropriation of African-American hip-hop culture: he wears a bandana and baggy pants and punctuates every sentence with "know 'm sayin."

Trailer Park Boys' depiction of this organic community rooted in white trash images appeared during a complex moment in Halifax's cultural and racial history. At the same time as writers such as George Elliott Clarke and others were radically redrawing the boundaries of what counts as Nova Scotia literature and willing the imaginative space of Africadia into existence,[5] Nova Scotia's status as the "Mississippi of the North" gained further notoriety, with high-profile incidents like a 2006 arson at the Black Loyalist Heritage Society in Birchtown and a 2010 cross-burning in Windsor, calling attention to the province's continued problems with segregation and racial intolerance (Perreaux 2010). With these long-standing anxieties surrounding race in the city and the province as a backdrop, Trailer Park Boys constructs an organic community rooted in images of white trash culture.

In her 2011 article "Speaking about the Nation: Critiques from the Canadian Margins," Michele Byers argues that "the series introduces the often invisible African Nova Scotian population to the screen but uses this introduction to cover over the deeply racist histories that keep Halifax one of the most segregated cities in Canada" (Byers 2011, 149). She goes on to suggest that "we could also read Julian and Ricky's feelings of at home-ness as precisely a product of white male privilege in what is often imagined to be (regional) white space within the nation ... because of the way Atlantic Canada often figures within national and transnational imaginaries, we might consider that *tpb*, or Sunnyvale, stands as one of the last places where white men are still king, the last of the truly white settler spaces" (150). *Trailer Park Boys* couches its representation of Sunnyvale in transgressive yet always ironic images of white trash culture. As I outline in more detail below, this construction of white innocence is particularly effective in Canada, where a diffuse white, anglophone culture forms what critical race theorists call a neutral backdrop against which "other" ethnic groups are judged (See Jiwani 2006; Mackey 2002; among others), and in Nova Scotia, where the pushback against the romanticized Scottish culture Ian McKay and others describe has created alienation and uncertainty about the link between regional identity and ethnicity. In this sense, images of white trash in *Trailer Park Boys* and other texts serve to anchor ideas surrounding race and regional identity.

Poor Boy's Game

Clement Virgo's 2007 film *Poor Boy's Game* also explores racial and class tensions in Halifax, portraying a white former teen boxing star, Donnie Rose, who, along with his brother, committed a vicious assault on his African Nova Scotian opponent, Charlie Carvery, when he was a teenager. Donnie later reveals to Charlie's father, George, that the attack was racially motivated, as he and his brother blamed the loss on the match's black referee. The film opens with Donnie being released from prison and attempting to reintegrate with his family and community. The assault and its aftermath – Charlie ended up with lingering mental deficiencies as a result of the beating – divide the community sharply along racial lines, as tensions quickly emerge between Donnie and his friends and members of the black community. Charlie's parents and congregants of their church meet to discuss their strong opposition to Donnie's release and possible methods of revenge; however, their plans are hijacked by another local boxer named Ozzy Paris, who offers to fight Donnie in the ring as a way to avenge the racially motivated attack.

Poor Boy's Game deals with many of the same themes as *Trailer Park Boys* (and also, incidentally, stars Corey Bowles), but approaches them in a much different way. Like *Trailer Park Boys*, *Poor Boy's Game* explores tensions over family and community in contemporary Halifax. The racial tensions in the film are, however, much more visceral: the young men are angry, disaffected, and out of work and the clash between the "rednecks" (which is what Ozzy calls Donnie) and the black community is at all times on the brink of violence. In her 2011 article, "'Boxing ain't no game': Clement Virgo's *Poor Boy's Game* as Canadian Racial

Counter-narrative," Andrea Medovarski argues that the film "dramatizes racial tensions in Halifax, perhaps one of the most racially segregated cities in this country, and its visual imagery foregrounds the ways this racism has its roots in centuries of slavery, violence, exclusion, and marginalization" (Medovarski 2011, 118–19). The film's violence is closely related to its portrayal of incarceration, the fall of the region's working-class culture, and surveillance, as members of the community keep tabs on one another and threaten to go to the police over parole violations. The film troubles traditional markers of masculinity; scenes in which Donnie trains, fights, and hones his body appear alongside him having consensual sex with his cell mate and his friends teasing him about being in prison, asking him if he still "likes pussy."

The film explores these tensions through depictions of crime and violence but also through changing patterns of work. George at first opposes Donnie being released from prison and even threatens him with a gun. He later comes around, however, and participates in training Donnie for the big fight against the wishes of the other members of his family and his community. In addition to his role in the fight, George is an important figure because he works at the docks. The film constructs a generational divide in which the dock workers are all the same age as George and the young men Donnie's age either have no work or make money as drug dealers or as bouncers. When Ozzy offers Donnie money for the fight he specifically ties the purse to a year's wages at the docks, at once calling attention to how little money is to be made there and insulting Donnie by rubbing in the fact that work at the docks is likely unavailable to him.

Like *Trailer Park Boys*, the film examines masculinity and ethnicity through the lens of the region's fading working-class culture: Donnie, his friends, and the men they clash with have very few prospects and seem always to end up either working at or going to a club that his uncle owns. His uncle openly discriminates against black customers and foments these tensions by challenging Donnie's masculinity and his commitment to family and to his community, at one point yelling that "About the only thing any of us have in this fucking world is our fucking tribe. The fucking niggers understand that. Why don't you?" The film strips away traditional markers of identity, including those that centre on work and masculinity. In this way, *Poor Boy's Game* and other boxing-related cultural products like Joel Thomas Hynes's *Little Dog* (cbc 2018) reduce recently incarcerated men to literally fighting for scraps and using only their battered bodies to survive.

Perhaps the most interesting thing about *Trailer Park Boys* is that although it is set in Halifax, the show could take place in any deindustrialized site in North America and the show goes to great lengths to strip away cues about its location. *Poor Boy's Game* goes the opposite way, peppering the film with street references (like Gottingen and Robie), showing Donnie running along a mostly deserted harbour, and highlighting the city's distinctive bridges. Just as *Trailer Park Boys* seasons always begin with Ricky leaving jail, *Poor Boy's Game* explores the connection between deindustrialization and the rise of the carceral state, depicting a world in which a group of out-of-work young men are always on the verge of being sent to jail. In this case, however, the action of the film is grounded in the specific space and history of Halifax, connecting the film more directly with other works like the 1999 experimental documentary *Welcome to Africville* and the writings of George Elliott Clarke and Maxine Tynes.

When the Saints

Trailer Park Boys's aggressive portrayal of the infantilized and degenerate Sunnyvale is contemporary Nova Scotia's gold standard for the transgressive version of white trash culture I outline in this chapter. Sarah Mian's *When the Saints* addresses many of the same themes. The novel is primarily about the main character, Tabby, returning to her hometown and attempting to reconcile with her dysfunctional family. While she is there, a bizarre kidnapping incident takes place in which an enemy of her brother and sister abducts her nephew, Swimmer. Tabby's succinct description of the incident provides a good sense of the overall tone of the novel: "[Swimmer] was taken by this low-life Troy whose teenage cousin was knocked up by my brother and almost died from having a rusty coat hanger rammed up her hoo-ha. Now, you'd think that putting my other brother in a wheelchair and getting me hooked on crack would be payback enough, but you know how it is with guys like Troy" (Mian 2015, 230). Like Sunnyvale, Mian's ironically named Jubilant is populated with violent con artists who seem to stand in stark contrast to McKay's portrait of the folk. Tabby's dry, nonchalant narration adds to the novel's sense of irony; like *Trailer Park Boys*, it dwells in the juxtaposition between expectations of what Nova Scotia might look like and a degraded representation of the region.

When the Saints opens with Tabby's first impressions of Jubilant and her anxieties about seeing her estranged family for the first time in years. She quickly discovers that in the time since she has been away, the already-dysfunctional Saints have fallen completely apart: her sister, an addict, struggles to support her children as a prostitute and the brother paralyzed in the incident described above lives in a filthy unlicensed group home.

Tabby is very conflicted about her family and about her hometown: while she has found some semblance of peace with them, she wants to turn away from all aspects of her background. Her sense of alienation from home and from her identity is exacerbated by the denatured and mainly abandoned space of Jubilant. She finds that the town, of which she has few good memories in the first place, is in the midst of a dramatic period of decay. This is particularly true of her childhood home, destroyed by a flood and left behind by her family: "Grandpa's shotguns are rusted out and there's a lonesome smell of oil over everything. The dirt floor next to the deep-freeze Daddy used to throw chunks of deer meat into is stained black from years of spilled blood. The wall hook is empty ... My boots on the floorboards set off a chain reaction of groans and rattles throughout the whole house. In the murky green light, everything looks like it's under water. The hallway is a jungle of coat hangers and unraveled cassette tapes, piles of fallen plaster and broken Christmas-tree ornaments" (Mian 2015, 2–3). After visiting the house, Tabby walks around the rest of the town and takes stock of how it has deteriorated in her absence. The streets are strewn with garbage and the town's dumpsters are covered in decades-old graffiti. Tabby notes that the downtown is particularly grim, with many of the businesses either boarded up or sporting bars on their windows (42).

Tabby connects the town's material decay with the region's economic prospects, particularly the end of its extractive and industrial activities at the close of the twentieth century. She notices the absence of the "breeze [that] always smelled like the car factory" (Mian 2015, 15) she remembers from growing up, talks about the collapse of the area's lobster fishery, and resents the town's shift to the service sector, remarking that the only businesses that seem to be open are struggling restaurants, which sell fake lobster, and shops that sell tacky items for tourists. At one point, Tabby sarcastically asks a shop if they "need someone to handpaint *Bay of Fundy* on all those conch shells they import from the Bahamas" (52).

Mian's depiction of postindustrial Nova Scotia capitalizes on the brand of transgressive white trash images popularized by *Trailer Park Boys*. Tabby's family is in complete disarray. Tabby reports, for example, that her sister Poppy has built toys and a playground for her children out of rusted and abandoned car parts, which are strewn around her backyard. Tabby's painful recollections of her childhood also feature white trash tropes surrounding domestic violence, poverty, and the humiliation of "wearing" the scars of these incidents in public: she remembers that her father broke her tooth when she was a little girl and that she had to refrain from smiling comfortably throughout her entire childhood until a "welfare dentist" fixed it when she was fifteen.

Much of the text focuses on how the evidence of violence and poverty – scars, dirty clothes, smells, poor nutrition – become public. Just as *Trailer Park Boys* is premised on putting this excessive version of white trash culture on display for the wider world (the conceit of the show is that filmmakers are shooting this footage for a documentary), *When the Saints* focuses on moments where such images appear in very public settings: "The Jubilant Day Queen has a big hickey on her neck, which didn't make her think twice about an updo. She waves to the crowd in white gloves like she's been doing this her whole life. As if Ma and I didn't just see her half an hour ago bumming change outside the liquor store, screeching to someone in a car, "Where's Jimmy at? He said he was getting hash for the Gravitron!" (Mian 2015, 211). This parade also features out of work lobster fishermen who pass through on a float decorated to look like an Employment Insurance (ei) line-up. Tabby's assessment of the town continually comes back to these images: the streets are filled with violent outbursts, the only convenience store in town prominently advertises that it cashes ei cheques and, reflecting on the town deciding to change the name of the street she grew up on to "Victory Road," Tabby notes that the "only victory I know of on this road involved a court battle over whether it's sanitary to run a daycare out of a barn" (114).

Like much literature and popular culture of Nova Scotia's postindustrial era, Mian's *When the Saints* flips the preoccupation with genetics and the family around. Instead of being a source of pride or a force that draws reluctant children into traditional activities (think, for example, of MacLeod's "The Boat" [1976]), family ties implicate Tabby and her siblings in a history of chaos: in elementary school, a classmate started a rumour that her mother and father were actually brother and sister (Mian 2015, 9), she often describes herself as "damaged goods" because of her family's heritage (24), and even refers to her grandfather as a "sort of hillbilly clairvoyant" because of his success in selling medicine made from "pig's blood and tree sap" (18).

Much of Tabby's recounting of her family history returns to the idea that she and her siblings are "marked" as Saints and that no matter how hard they try to reject the lifestyle their parents and grandparents passed down to them (especially her father's penchant for scamming their neighbours),[6] their genetic makeup will always prevail. While this family history essentially led to the Saints being forcibly removed from Jubilant, it also carries over to other parts of Tabby's life. She references an incident in which she was romantically involved with a Mi'kmaq man whom she moved in with; however, she was eventually asked to leave the reserve because she was not a member of the community. Tabby's sense of alienation from every community she has ever tried to join leads her to come back to her family, almost against her will. She says, "I wonder if there really is such a thing as blood ties. Even though I always thought of my family as just a pack of wolves forced to live together in that big drafty shack, I do feel something pull on me every now and then" (Mian 2015, 42). Elsewhere, after she is denied a job she has expressed interest in because of her last name, she reflects, "If ever I drifted just an inch from being a Saint, something always snapped me back in my place" (7).

Mian is interested in many of the questions familiar from earlier generations of Nova Scotia writers. While MacLeod's fiction is about threats to community and tradition in the modern world, *When the Saints*, *Trailer Park Boys*, and other depictions of postindustrial Nova Scotia take the destruction and loss of those ideas as their starting point. In spite of this, Mian and others continue to be interested in core questions about identity and community and examine the way in which concepts such as environmental and genetic determinism play out in such a denatured and trash-strewn world.

Perhaps unsurprisingly, then, *When the Saints*, like much of Coady's early fiction and *Trailer Park Boys*, ends on a decidedly nostalgic and hopeful note. Tabby's anxieties about her family history fade away at the end of the novel, as she enters into a stable relationship with the rest of the Saints. After recovering Swimmer and unexpectedly receiving a large sum of money from her father, Tabby and her family move to Solace River together. The novel's satiric approach to the service industry also softens at the end, as a call centre moves in and provides stability both to the community and to the Saints: Jackie finds a job on the construction crew building the call centre and Tabby eventually gets a job making calls.

Just beneath My Skin

Darren Greer's *Just beneath My Skin* also depicts a deindustrialized Nova Scotia community marked by pollution and disarray. In Greer's North River, the local mill has all but died out and the river is full of foamy sludge, which has killed off the gaspereau. As the title of the novel would suggest, *Just beneath My Skin* is focused on anxieties around bloodlines, especially the relationship between the two main characters, Jake and his son Nathan. The book jacket itself speaks to the importance of genetics in the novel, advertising it in the following terms: "The dying town of North River is a place where poverty, violence, and despair are passed down like original sin from generation to generation." Like *When the Saints*, *Just beneath My Skin* plays on white trash tropes in constructing this "fallen" version of Nova Scotia: the characters abuse alcohol and drugs, engage in outlandish feuds that end in gun violence, and argue over paternity. Carla calls Jake's father a "white trash minister" (Greer 2014, 193).

The narrative focus oscillates between Jake and Nathan; each chapter switches to the other's point of view and the reader gets two versions of parts of the story as a result. Jake and Nathan have a complicated relationship. Jake is reluctant to acknowledge that he has a son and so Nathan must navigate a delicate situation in which he is unable to speak about this issue with either his mother or his father and where Jake gives him vague hints but leaves things ultimately unsaid. This changes when Jake returns to North River and deems Nathan's mother to be unfit, because she drinks heavily and is physically abusive toward her son.

The two major events of the narrative are Jake's attempts to gain custody of Nathan and Jake's friend, Johnny, hunting him down in a drug-addled haze as retribution for leaving North River in the first place. The main characters repeatedly come back to the idea that, for better or worse, your identity is imprinted on you at birth: Nathan and Jake spend much of the novel piecing together their family history and Johnny's vendetta against Jake comes down to him being offended that his friend moved to Halifax, left the supposedly tightknit community of North River behind, and in effect tried to become someone he is not; he asks, "Who says you get to get away, McNeil? Who says you're so much better than the rest?" (Greer 2014, 166).

Like Mian's Jubilant and Coady's Port Hawkesbury, Greer's North River is reeling from shifts in the extractive economy. Jake imagines the ghosts of his grandfather's generation logging on the river and Nathan finds it hard to believe that the river once sustained a forestry industry because "in the summer below the mill [the river] stinks of sulphur and foam clings to the banks as thick and yellow as pus" (Greer 2014, 10). The postextractive economy is just as hard on the residents of North River as it is on Mian's characters. Nathan reports that everyone who lives on his street is on social assistance and Jake notes that almost all of his friends have stopped working at the mill and have turned to selling drugs.

The trappings of the industrial era are appealing for nostalgic portraits of Canada's east coast: the masculine culture of work, the continuity of family and community through shared experience and sometimes trauma, and the almost fetishistic treatment of commodities like coal and fish. Images and stories about dragging things out of the ground also necessarily connect communities with the land, which feeds into Canadian literature's preoccupation with environmental determinism and settler society's search for home in the alien space of North America (Atwood 1972; Chalykoff 2000; Frye 1971; McGregor 1985; Sugars 2004). Jake is particularly concerned with the idea of emerging from and returning to the land, a fantasy often linked to postcolonial anxieties about the tenuous relationship between Canadian settler society and the natural environment. Jake reports that his grandfather was part of what he imagined to be an elemental folk culture that was intimately connected with the landscape. Although his grandfather was "an uneducated, ungodly fool of a man with barely two teeth in his head and a too-simple heart" (Greer 2014, 7), Jake also remembers stories about his masterful ability to "ride and roll the logs ... poling and prodding the ones that hung up on the banks or that slowed and gathered in creases in the eddies" (8). Upon his return from the war, his grandfather kissed the ground and swore he would never leave Nova Scotia again – a promise he managed to keep (179). Jake also tells a story about his grandmother saving herself and his father from a deadly forest fire that ravaged the area by hiding for several days underground in a well only to emerge from the earth unscathed.[7] His fearful dreams about Johnny's impending attack lead him back to this preoccupation with forging an authentic and unassailable identity through a connection with the land. He worries, for example, that Johnny is planning to "throw [him] into the swamp to be sucked into the ground like a stone" (78).

Like *When the Saints*, *Just beneath My Skin* employs brief references to the Mi'kmaq community as a way of establishing the boundaries of the white community that is its focus. Tabby's inability to find acceptance on the reserve accentuates her alienation from every other community she has ever tried to join. Jake and Nathan, on the other hand, bring up their Indigenous bloodline as a way to consolidate their own narrative of belonging while preserving their white heritage: "I found out later my grandmother, who wanted my father to become a preacher, was born on the reserve, though she was adopted into a white family in North River when she was young and didn't admit to coming from Wildcat at all … 'Your grandmother don't like to talk about it, and I'll be a crossed goose if I ever held it against a woman where she come from or whose people she was born into. But she was raised white, which is what counts'" (Greer 2014, 101). *Just beneath My Skin* is similar to *When the Saints* and *Trailer Park Boys* in that confused or incomplete narratives of genetic lineage are ultimately reconciled in straightforward and conventional ways. Belonging always means being part of a white community, even if that community is marked by disorder on the surface. In this case, Jake's grandfather openly talks about that white culture bringing in his wife and creating order not just for her but for the family's bloodline.

Nathan has a similar level of confidence about his ancestry, in spite of the fact that Jake is largely absent from his life and refuses to speak openly about their relationship. In a passage that combines postcolonial anxieties about springing up from the ground with stereotypes about the culture of Atlantic Canada, Nathan recalls kids from his school teasing him about the absence of his father during presentations about their families:

After that the kids started saying I didn't have any father. They said a seagull jerked off on a rock and the sun hatched me. I didn't know what jerked off was so I asked Jake …

"I wouldn't worry about those assholes in your class," Jake said. "You know who your father is, don't you?"
"Yes, Jake."
"That's all that matters then," Jake said.
That was the closest Jake and I ever came to talking about it. (Greer 2014, 46–7)

Like Mian, Greer softens the edges of his deconstruction of the family and community under the conditions of Nova Scotia's postindustrial economic and social structure. On the surface, the novel, like *Trailer Park Boys,* seems to be about the disintegration of the family that mirrors the fall of North River, but the novel filters this sense of decay, at both a physical and social level, through a nostalgic commitment to coherent ideas about family, community, and, ultimately, race.

The novel's final sequence returns to and resolves these anxieties around the family. Nathan gets a degree of closure about his family ties as the novel progresses, as he goes to live with Jake and his grandfather to get away from his mother's erratic behaviour. In the final pages, Jake's father and Nathan find Johnny about to shoot Jake during a violent confrontation. Johnny eventually turns the gun on Nathan and his grandfather, but Jake intervenes and even takes a bullet for his son and his father. The final lines strike a nostalgic and almost pastoral tone, with Nathan's last descriptions of North River switching from the polluted and violent early accounts to "moons and stars and indigo skies and blueberries and trout and lowing cattle and Ferris wheels" (Greer 2014, 216). More importantly, Jake and Nathan come to terms with their complicated relationship, although much remains unsaid. Jake's final lines reflect his inability to communicate: "The last thing I see is the face of my son, staring at me, looking like he is about to cry. The last thing I see is the face of my son. I am your father, I want to say. But I have no voice" (14). And Nathan's final lines similarly suggest that the questions about genetic lineage and family that persist through the novel are tied off, even if he still calls Jake by his first name: "I don't cry. Jake would be real proud of me" (217).

***

Contemporary Nova Scotian literature and popular culture's disaffection with the tartan paradigm intersects with a wider backlash against political correctness and liberal multiculturalism coursing throughout the Anglosphere (given voice by Donald Trump, Jeremy Clarkson, and the Ford brothers). This general ambivalence about race manifests itself in articulations of rural culture throughout Canada. In her work on emerging expressions of "redneck pride," Anne O'Connell argues that Canada is marked by a tension between urban areas (which are supposedly diverse and tolerant) and rural areas (which are supposedly homogeneous and regressive). For her, this distinction between rural and urban fits nicely into Canada's narrative of "unity through diversity": rural areas stand as symbols of tradition and the country's pioneering spirit (always crucially connected to an empty land) characteristic of the founding values of Canada, while cities showcase the modern, liberal values that illustrate the country's diversity (O'Connell 2010, 538). O'Connell notes that the term "redneck," once "part of a pollution ideology that helped police the boundaries between the white working-class and white middle class" (O'Connell 2010, 545), has been reclaimed in North American popular culture (think *Duck Dynasty* and *Here Comes Honey Boo Boo*) and political discourse (think Sarah Palin). She notes that the reclaiming of this term is connected to other movements waged by angry white males whose prominence in the political sphere is threatened and who feel alienated and marginalized by multiculturalism and political correctness.

Sunnyvale, Virgo's Halifax, Jubilant, and North River complicate received ideas about family, community, and ethnicity in postindustrial Nova Scotia. These texts push back against the tartan paradigm that McKay describes, but also against the articulation of Scottish culture found in the work of MacLeod and other earlier writers. Like *Trailer Park Boys*, the work of Mian and Greer constructs a dysfunctional portrait of postindustrial Nova Scotia that plays on white trash stereotypes. In each of these texts, characters are ambivalent about their genetic backgrounds, and the landscape they share is denatured, abandoned, and covered in trash. While the violence, drug use, and general alienation featured in *When the Saints*, *Just beneath My Skin*, *Trailer Park Boys*, and even Coady's work seems to be a radical departure from previous generations of Nova Scotian authors, this material is often filtered through nostalgic ideas about the continuity of family and a connection to the landscape.

5

Cottonland and *Oxyana*: Prescription Drugs and Moral Panics

Early in the morning of 12 October 2013, Shane Edward Matheson stabbed Scott Jones, a gay musician and activist based in New Glasgow, as Jones walked from one bar to another on Archimedes Street. This was the second Thanksgiving weekend in three years in which New Glasgow, a small community of around 10,000 people on Nova Scotia's North Shore, witnessed acts of seemingly random violence at that particular bar (Dooley's, which would later be renamed Acro Lounge), the earlier one being the kidnapping and murder of nineteen-year-old Amber Kirwan in 2011. The response to both incidents followed a very similar pattern. Rather than focusing on complex and systemic issues surrounding homophobia, a lack of safe space in Pictou County, or a prevalence of gender-based violence in the community, much of the media attention focused on the perpetrators' (Matheson and in the case of Kirwin, Chris Falconer) mental health and drug use (including prescription drug use), at once providing a straightforward and easy-to-digest explanation for the events and a framework for thinking of them as isolated incidents (Harvie 2014a, 2014b).

Consider the image on the front page of *The News* the day after the Scott Jones stabbing. The photo of the Roseland Cabaret is striking for several reasons: the bar itself looks like an abandoned and boarded up factory (it is actually a repurposed theatre built in 1913)[1]; there is a distinctive stain on the ground where authorities cleaned up Jones's blood, and perhaps most jarring, the marquee above the bodily fluids and disinfectant advertises a performance by a band called Zombie Apocalypse. There is a lot to say here about the stubborn refusal of traumatic events to be wiped away (a key theme in this book), about changes in the physical landscape of northern Nova Scotia that accompany the shift from the industrial to the postindustrial eras, and about the nature of Pictou County's public space in general.

In this chapter, I focus specifically on the phrase "Zombie Apocalypse," although I will be judicious in the way I employ this metaphor. The stabbing took place in the context of a growing sense of unease surrounding contagion and drugs in northern Nova Scotia. Some of the specific responses to the incident focused on the idea that places like downtown New Glasgow had become breeding grounds for violence fuelled by prescription and other drugs. Earlier in 2013, for example, New Glasgow was home to what was believed to be the largest seizure of bath salts in the history of Canada (*The News* 2013). In addition to New Glasgow's troubles with bath salts, places like Glace Bay, Sydney, and other parts of the province's postindustrial belt have been hit hard by the rise of prescription drug abuse. In its coverage of drug use in the region, the mainstream media openly creates a sense of panic and frames the issue as a kind of contagion, referring to oxycontin and other opiates as "hillbilly heroin," talking about the "spread" of the problem of drug addiction from the United States and other parts of the region, and publishing stories about prescription drug addicts stealing from their own relatives and turning into violent, zombie-like versions of themselves after being exposed to the drugs (cbc News 2003; Richer 2003). More nuanced treatments of the rise of prescription drug abuse in these areas consider these practices byproducts of the industrial era, since there is a history of overprescribing pain medication to miners and other workers.

In this chapter, I consider the way in which ideas such as drug use, pollution, and the destruction of communities and the bodies of users intersect with northern Nova Scotia's struggle to reconcile the fall of the industrial era. I suggest that this discourse is indicative of a general shift in Nova Scotia's culture and that it is related to the emergence of white trash as an identity marker in the postindustrial era. This articulation of images of white trash culture

5.1 Roseland Cabaret, 12 October 2013

intersects with concepts surrounding pollution, contagion, and the degrading of the white working-class body by drugs.

Most of the chapters so far have at least indirectly addressed images of the body and the relationship between the body and the physical environment. The body is a key site for understanding postindustrial culture. Cultural producers, media reports, and even the commemorative industry constantly return to images of the body, as the body conveys ideas about gender and work, is impacted by toxins and other pollutants, and is labelled white trash in certain postindustrial spaces. This chapter looks at the way these ideas circulate in the 2006 documentary *Cottonland*, which examines the rise of prescription drug abuse in Glace Bay. I consider the way in which prescription drug abuse is framed as a contagion – in one of the key moments in the documentary, a local doctor argues that oxycontin use swept up the eastern seaboard to Cape Breton from the southern Appalachians like a virus – and as a form of pollution in the supposedly idyllic space of Nova Scotia. To make this point, I read *Cottonland* against a similar documentary, *Oxyana* (2013), which explores the same issues in a small community in West

Virginia. Reading the documentaries together brings into focus the extent to which anxieties about prescription drug abuse signal broader fears surrounding changes in patterns of work, threats to tradition, and the degenerate body, all of which are symbols of the decline of the industrial era.[2]

PRESCRIPTION DRUGS AS POLLUTION

There is a link between the rise of prescription drug abuse in Nova Scotia and the rise of depictions of white trash in both the media and popular culture. Both are wrapped up in complex ideas surrounding contagion and pollution and both contribute to *Cottonland*'s depiction of industrial Cape Breton as a toxic zone. *Cottonland* and many of the texts I am working with suggest that the working-class body in postindustrial Nova Scotia is at risk. While working-class men in the industrial era were at risk of being crushed in mines or injured in factories, the working-class body in postindustrial Nova Scotia is at risk of pollution both from toxins left behind after the industrial era and, as I discuss in this chapter, through exposure to drug use and a constellation of other impurities. *Cottonland* in particular relies on an almost nostalgic juxtaposition between the pure and clean working-class bodies and natural environment of the industrial era and the destroyed, defiled, and impure bodies and landscapes of the postindustrial era.

In her 2010 book, *Bodily Natures: Science, Environment, and the Material Self*, Stacy Alaimo suggests that the type of attention that *Cottonland* pays to the intersection between the body and the toxic landscape is common in literature and popular culture of the postindustrial era. She argues that in a world overrun with hard-to-detect chemicals, toxins, and pesticides, the body becomes the "literal contact zone between human corporeality and more-than-human nature" (Alaimo 2010, 2). While much of the environmental cultural studies scholarship of the 1990s and 2000s viewed nature as a social construction,[3] Alaimo suggests that by attending to the materiality of the body, literary and cultural studies scholars can better understand the degree to which it is enmeshed in the world around us in often immeasurable and invisible ways. Alaimo notes that since chemicals constantly seep into the soil where we grow our food and into the water we drink, chemical agents and toxins are increasingly connected with biological bodies. She argues that this brings us to "a more uncomfortable place where the 'human' is always already part of an active, often unpredictable material world" in which we understand that toxins and other contaminants have seeped into all of our bodies and that the pollutants and other unwanted material we try to manage through remediation are "already within" (18).

Many cultural studies and literary scholars working on this concept pay close attention to the impact of pollution and what is often called "toxic consciousness" (Buell 1998, Deitering 1996, Heise 2002) on marginalized communities and countries – a process that Rob Nixon has eloquently called "slow violence" (Nixon 2011). *Toxic Tourism: Rhetorics of Pollution, Travel, and Environmental Justice* (2007), Phaedra Pezzullo's provocative project of taking leisure trips to polluted environments, speaks to the limits of relying on visual evidence of toxicity. Toxins are elusive: they are often undetectable, and the fact that toxic environments predominantly affect racialized and marginalized communities and are deliberately kept out of view makes them difficult to "see." Equally significantly, Pezzullo argues that Western culture has shifted from registering profound shock at the prevalence of chemicals (think of the stir caused by publication of *Silent Spring* in 1962) to a kind of passive acceptance in which chemicals and their effects are viewed as a banal part of contemporary existence. She writes, "Largely due to their excessive scale, obscurity, and overall danger, toxins often appear surreal for those of us who do not live, work, or play in or near toxic facilities or dumps on a daily basis" (Pezzullo 2007, 60). She goes on to argue that toxins are especially problematic for the cultural imagination because they offer both "dreams (of science, technology, and upward mobility) and nightmares (of insignificance, fallibility, and illness)" (60).

Countries with advanced industrial economies such as Canada rely heavily on keeping the visual evidence of these polluted spaces out of the way. The environmental and human toll of the Alberta oil sands, for example, is at least partially mitigated by its remote location. In the case of Canada's Chemical Valley (Sarnia, Ontario), Sarah Wiebe suggests that these kinds of spaces – we have different words for them: marginal, precarious, overexploited, sacrifice zones, toxic environments – constitute situations where people live with "their bodies on the line" (Wiebe 2010, 1). For Wiebe, these precarious zones are the strongest examples of Lefebvre's and others' assertion that space is not a neutral backdrop for the actions of human society. She argues that "this space is not a dead or passive space; rather the spaces of liminality I discuss produce meanings and experiences that are revealing about the state of politics at the local/global interface" (2). For Wiebe, these spaces also break down national boundaries, as toxins and air pollution travel across large distances, often undetected: "In toxic environments ... borders become de-territorialized; yet, the body internalizes territories through the infiltration of invisible harm in the form of toxic exposure" (2).

For my purposes, the key observation here is the connection between the degraded toxic landscape and the bodies of the people who live in these spaces. Wiebe argues that representations of these precarious zones in literature, popular culture, and the media often include moral judgments about the people who live there. These assessments often rely on binary distinctions such as clean and dirty, secure and insecure, local and global, internal and external, and of course nature and culture – boundaries that toxic zones call into question. Such judgments can be negative (for example, linking cancer rates or other diseases to lifestyle choices and poor diet, or connecting pollution to a certain willingness to be abused) or "positive" (for example, calling attention to the history of bravery and sacrifice in postindustrial areas). Wiebe, Sherene Razack, and others argue that it is important to contest this reading of such marginalized spaces; within them "bodies are simultaneously infiltrated with toxins and discursive meanings" (Wiebe 2010, 8). Images of white trash culture capture this simultaneous infiltration of the body with toxins and discursive meanings very effectively.

In their article "'This is your face on meth': The Punitive Spectacle of White Trash in the Rural War on Drugs" (2013), Travis Linnemann and Tyler Wall point out that drug abuse makes for a compelling image of pollution in such toxic spaces. They argue that rural drug users often appear in documentaries, news reports, and public service announcements (psas) as "'shadow people' … a nascent criminal class, plaguing lands where 'traditional life' is supposedly 'valued most'" (Linnemann and Wall 2013, 316). Linnemann and Wall suggest that this focus on the prevalence of drug abuse in rural settings and the panic associated with it often obscures even more complex issues such as declining populations, outmigration, uneven regional development, and environmental degradation. Like horror films (Carroll 1987, 52), these documentaries and psas accentuate the "normality" or health of the communities prior to the arrival of these practices, framing the rise of drug addiction as a kind of plague or epidemic.

Linnemann and Wall go on to argue that the faces and bodies of drug users in postindustrial contexts form a set of abject images that play on the fears of "mainstream society"; they access "several intertwined bourgeois anxieties, namely binaries of cleanliness and filth, attractiveness and ugliness, productive and unproductive labor, inclusion and exclusion … [these images] are structured by and embedded within long-standing cultural-economic anxieties about the figure of 'white trash' and the dominance and precariousness of white social position" (Linnemann and Wall 2013, 321). Linnemann and Wall suggest that the fears surrounding rural drug addiction are wrapped up with anxieties surrounding race in parts of rural North America: "abject horrors built into the imaginary of methamphetamine are not simply about crossing juridical boundaries, but also about defiling and polluting one's own body, a white body in particular" (325). Unlike cocaine and even socially acceptable prescription drugs such as vicodin, oxy's are labelled as nonrecreational and low-rent. The opioid crisis has become a state of emergency, and while its effects are widely seen in cities such as Ottawa and Vancouver, much of the discourse in North American media has focused on its effects on rural and postindustrial areas, especially Appalachia and the rust belt.[4] As the name "hillbilly heroin" suggests, these drugs are considered to be more destructive than their mainstream counterparts; they are produced in an amateurish and backward fashion, often in tubs or sheds.

The image of these drugs is complicated for a place like Atlantic Canada; on the one hand they run counter to the conventional idea of innocence and reverence for tradition (whatever that means) we usually associate with life in the region, but more importantly, they fit into the second side of the folk paradigm that Wyile identifies: the degenerate, backward, incestuous, and ultimately destructive version of the folk.

Prescription drug use offers a particularly powerful set of abject images. Ostensibly, these drugs are designed to heal people or at least make them feel better; however, in stripping them, cooking them, and then injecting them, addicts find a way to use these drugs to destroy their bodies in very visible ways and make themselves much worse off. Significantly, North American popular culture is littered with references to the destructive effects of methamphetamine, oxycontin, and other forms of "hillbilly heroin"; consider, for example, *30 Rock* (2006–13),[5] *The Wild and Wonderful Whites of West Virginia* (2009), and, of course, *Breaking Bad* (2008–13).

In *Odd Tribes: Toward a Cultural Analysis of White People* (2005), Hartigan argues that in *Deliverance* (1972), "white trash" images appear in what he calls a "tense narrative landscape in the zone between Nature and Culture" (Hartigan 2005, 137), specifically the intersection of one of the last undeveloped and uncontaminated rivers in the South and a mega-dam project that threatens it. He argues that the film and the images we associate with it are fuelled by this clash and that *Deliverance* is populated by primitive "'natives,' poor whites who live in a contaminated zone of junked yards. Referred to as hillbillies and mountain men, they represent an inability to become fully 'civilized' humans; their 'backward' location in the woods perversely confuses the boundary between Culture and Nature, problematized in this narrative by the conjunction of trash and natives" (137). I suggest that *Cottonland* and *Oxyana* take place in a similarly tense narrative landscape. The films rely on a juxtaposition of the purity of Nature (in the case of *Cottonland*, the gleaming landscape of Cape Breton, a place regularly voted one of the most beautiful tourist destinations in the world on the strength of its rugged coastline, mix of sea and mountain, and beautiful fall colours) and Culture (the landscape degraded by the presence of the region's industrial infrastructure: strip mines, abandoned industrial sites, fast food shops, and boarded up buildings) and on a relentless focus on the equally degraded bodies of drug users. Before I get there, it is worth mentioning that anxieties about drugs pop up elsewhere in the province's contemporary literature and popular culture.

In Coady's *Strange Heaven* (1998), for example, Bridget and her friends casually discuss a boy from their school committing suicide by overdosing on prescription drugs: "Darlene MacEachern's brother had driven out to Point Tupper and parked at a place where a lot of high school students come at night. It overlooked both the water and the mill, and so at night the white and yellow and red lights of the latter would twinkle sentimentally off the former. But this had been in the afternoon, in wintertime, and he had brought all his grandmother's painkillers for her cancer, which he swallowed with Orange Big 8" (Coady 1998, 45). This image brings together a number of issues relevant to postindustrial Nova Scotia: the possible link between cancer and the region's industrial areas (the unnamed town in *Strange Heaven* is home to a big mill, which pollutes both the water and the air), the dangerous role of prescription drugs in these communities, and the tension between industrial activities and the service industry (Darlene's father is "high up at the mill" and Big 8 is a Sobeys brand).

Virtually every storyline in *Trailer Park Boys* revolves around drugs, but the characters are almost exclusively engaged in using, growing, and selling marijuana. In season 8, Ricky, Julian, and Bubbles embark on a plan seemingly inspired by *Breaking Bad* in which they use a complicated refining process to turn a large batch of weed into "honey oil." In the same season, Bubbles is arrested for acting erratically in public; the police do so because they think he is on bath salts. While the show is generally lighthearted in its treatment of the characters' overuse of alcohol and drugs, it also plays on stereotypes about unemployed, violent, and erratic drug users. In spite of his efforts, Ricky is unable to hold down a job because his drug use trips up his plans and makes him incoherent. Ray and Lahey represent middle-aged versions of Ricky, as they have lost their jobs because of substance-abuse issues. Ray, who is involved in many of Ricky and Julian's schemes, fakes a disability and pretends to be in a wheelchair, evoking stereotypes about welfare fraud and alcoholism.

In contrast to these decidedly ambivalent representations of drug use in postindustrial Nova Scotia, Michelle Ferguson's 2013 novel *Why Here?* features an exaggerated panic over the arrival of meth in a small Nova Scotia community. The novel is heavy-handed in its treatment of this theme: Ian McKendrie moves to insular Potato Island from Toronto and begins to sell meth, leading to one of his friends, Rennie, becoming addicted, being assaulted, and breaking into a local pharmacy. Outraged at the prospect of their town being destroyed by drugs and at the lack of support they receive from the justice system, Rennie's father and some of his friends take the law into their own hands. They stage an elaborate *Weekend at Bernie's*-style scheme in which they conceal the death of the local chief of police, apprehend McKendrie, and hold him until a local couple has a chance to show him the concern he never received from his addict mother and he turns his life around. *Why Here?* draws a sharp portrait of the threat of drugs in the space of small-town Nova Scotia: characters recall a wholesome and down-to-earth community before McKendrie's arrival and argue that he single-handedly destroyed their town when he arrived and started selling drugs to its unsuspecting residents.

The novel explicitly employs the language of contagion I outline above in describing the effects of meth use on Rennie – a nice young boy who has turned into a zombie-like figure: "The swelling in Rennie's face had come down, so Arch could see when his eyes were opened. But he didn't know these vacant, hollowed-out eyes. Somewhere along the way, they had replaced his son's brilliant blue ones" (Ferguson 2013, 6). Throughout the novel, characters make excuses for Rennie, whom they see, in contrast to McKendrie, as a genuine member of the community who has simply made some bad choices. Hettie, whose store Rennie robbed, says, for example, "His eyes were something terrible ... Rennie had a hammer in his hand. It was Rennie, for sure, but when he looked up, he was no one I recognized" (194). In spite of this, Hettie cannot bring herself to press charges against him because of her relationship with his father: "I couldn't do that to Arch. He's been a dear friend, and I had to believe that the Rennie we all loved was still in there somewhere. I haven't seen him back yet, but I sure am hopeful" (195).

The same characters see McKendrie as a virus that needs to be eradicated and some literally campaign for him to be shot for bringing meth to the otherwise peaceful island. In *Why Here?* there is an overarching sense that drug use represents a threat not just to the individual but to the community as a whole. Furthermore, the threat goes beyond worries about increased crime and the general health and well-being of residents; the novel continually returns to the idea that this kind of behaviour disrupts an otherwise pristine and innocent way of life. The text achieves this in part by stressing memories of Potato Island before McKendrie's arrival. When Arch thinks back to the first time he saw him, for example, he recalls that McKendrie came off the ferry carrying a paper with "an ad about living the untouched life" (Ferguson 2013, 7). While there are moments where characters express frustration with the idea that this inauthentic version of regional culture serves as fodder for tourism ads, on the whole the novel conveys the sense that McKendrie is in the process of destroying an otherwise organic and idyllic community.

Many of the characters expressly frame the arrival of drugs to the island as a contagion. Beth, for example, says, "Truth is ... I don't think a one of us will ever be the same. It's like the poison that went into Rennie went into all of us. Changed us a little bit" (Ferguson 2013, 143). Clarence explicitly states that Beth is talking about more than simply the physical effects of the drugs: "I think that's right. A little bit of that world out there came on in and left its mark" (143). As I discuss in more detail below, the idea that drugs represent a kind of existential contagion within the space of postindustrial Nova Scotia is sustained in part by the prevalence of discourses about the infiltration of the region by the modern, overcivilized culture that McKay describes and then by tourists, as described in the work of later theorists and cultural producers (Wyile 2008). *Why Here?* and *Cottonland* rely on received images of Nova Scotia as "unspoiled" in portraying the impact of the spread of drugs in the province.

COTTONLAND AND OXYANA

Cottonland employs a visual strategy that implicitly creates binary distinctions between healthy and diseased, natural and polluted, vibrant and decaying. This is true from the opening moments, where the faces of the healthy miners found in old footage are immediately contrasted with the gaunt and twitchy faces of the addicts who populate the film. The film's establishing shots repeatedly come back to a degraded version of "Nature" that includes grey vacant lots, abandoned houses and buildings, power lines, and views of the bleak highway leading into Sydney. This sense of decay drives the film's narrative structure. The documentary opens with descriptions of the proud miners and vibrant pits of the early twentieth century and waxes nostalgic about a time when work in the mines kept communities together and men honest. The film overlays its depiction of the declining region with images of addicts who have gone from healthy to sick and who are being offered a chance at rehabilitation.

In his work on the emergence of the label "white trash" in northern states and the midwest, Hartigan argues that in the early twentieth century, the work of eugenicists contributed to the spread of these images by providing a quasi-scientific basis for the stereotypes they propagated (Hartigan 2005, 89). The same kind of logic is at play in *Cottonland* and *Oxyana*. These films employ medical professionals who talk about the genetic and health-related aspects of addiction. In this sense, the films solidify assumptions about white trash culture by appealing to scientific ideas; the people they feature are not simply degraded specimens of white culture; they have been identified, monitored, and labelled by medical professionals. Hartigan calls this an "explanatory framework" (77), as the general stereotypes surrounding white trash are bolstered by this medical information. He argues that in places like Detroit and Atlantic Canada, there is a latent anxiety about the idea that these kinds of behaviours are spreading and that white culture in these spaces is degenerating. By employing medical and scientific language, media reports and experts convey that these people are fundamentally and perhaps even biologically different from mainstream white culture and that it is incumbent upon these communities to stop the spread of this contagion. This language creeps into *Cottonland* and into news reports surrounding the rise of oxycontin addiction (and later the threat of bath salts) in Nova Scotia.

About halfway through *Cottonland*, the documentary's principal expert, Dr Tom Crawford, attempts to explain the prevalence of prescription drug use in Glace Bay. He cites a history of overprescribing painkillers to workers in the mines, the high incidence of cancer and other diseases potentially related to pollution from the industrial era, and genetic factors, including the high number of Scots-Irish descendants who, according to him, have a hereditary predisposition to addiction. In addition to these factors, Crawford mentions that prescription drug addiction is simply a feature of the postindustrial economy in general; he notes that miners often abused alcohol and it is unsurprising to him that their children would turn to prescription drugs. He also speculates that the rise of prescription drug abuse in Cape Breton is linked to the spread of this practice northward from the southern Appalachians to rural Nova Scotia. He says, "On the surface, we've had an explosion of the addict population using oxycontin. On a more profound level, we've experienced the tail end of an oxycontin epidemic that began in lower Appalachia and worked its way up and finally reached us … It's like a continental virus" (*Cottonland* 2006).

Without spending time either confirming or refuting Crawford's assertion that the wave of oxycontin drug abuse began in Appalachia and moved up the eastern seaboard, I would argue that this moment provides insight into Nova Scotia's specific experience of the impact of prescription drug abuse. The fear of oxycontin and other painkillers takes the form of a moral panic, in the sense that media coverage of it often relies on such unsubstantiated figures and ominous ideas. More significantly, Crawford's use of the word "virus" and his assertion that the oxy craze originated in the degenerate and backward Appalachian south (which fits in with the use of the term "hillbilly heroin" in the media) demonstrate that what is at stake here is more than the physical health of the community. *Cottonland* and many news stories frame the rise of prescription drugs as a threat to the identity of Nova Scotia's supposedly otherwise stable communities.

Linnemann and Wall argue that in these kinds of narratives, the bodies of addicts are mapped on to the communities in question. *Cottonland* often compares the decay of the bodies of Glace Bay's addicts and the more general decay of the community itself. The idea of the oxycontin addicts defiling their bodies through drug use is displaced over the entire community: the act of consuming these drugs is destructive not only to the addicts as individuals but also to the community as a whole. The destruction to the community is further highlighted by its picturesque setting and by received ideas surrounding Nova Scotia's innocence. In this sense, the images the audience encounters in *Cottonland* are compelling because they threaten a hegemonic idea of what Nova Scotian identity represents.

After establishing that Glace Bay was once a healthy and vibrant community, the documentary zeroes in on threats to the region's way of life: the closure of 160 mines over the past fifty years, the retreat of capital, outmigration, and most profoundly, according to the film, oxycontin abuse – a force that is destructive in very tangible and visible ways. In the decayed and decaying present, houses are falling apart and people are moving out of the crime-ridden community, but Glace Bay, like the addicts the film follows, has a chance at rehabilitation. The film's focus on the addict as a metaphor for industrial Cape Breton spills into other aspects of its analysis. Crawford claims that the experience of being addicted to drugs is not unlike the economic history of a region that relied on industries that constantly needed government bailouts to survive. He says, "There's kind of an analogy between a dependent economy and a dependent person."

Cottonland eventually advances Membertou First Nation, a community that in 2006 was in the process of starting a number of infrastructure projects and recruiting people back to the region, as a model for Glace Bay. The timeline of rehabilitation for both the addicts and the region itself follows this pattern: the mines close, once-productive men and their children turn to prescription drugs, the region shifts to a focus on service industries, and methadone clinics offer a path out of prescription drug abuse. Fears surrounding the epidemic of drug use in Nova Scotia are symptomatic of a broader set of anxieties surrounding the pollution of the province's cultural identity. As *Cottonland* makes clear, the oxycontin scare maps easily on to other fears about the region's culture being degraded: specifically, the loss of jobs in extractive and manufacturing industries for working-class men; the fall of industry and the rise of the service sector; pollution and the destruction of the region's landscape; lingering effects of the industrial era on the body, especially fears about cancer; outmigration (one of the implicit problems with prescription addiction is that it means that people who suffer from it are ineligible to work out west in other extractive industries); and the infection of regional identity by white trash or hillbilly culture from other parts of North America.

Unlike cocaine spreading into the United States from Mexico and Colombia, oxycontin is not imported illegally to Nova Scotia; rather than the drugs themselves travelling from the south, it is the act of using them recreationally and the lifestyle associated with these activities that have moved in. As I have discussed several times in this book, there is a wide range of fears about this connection between a broadly defined American south and Nova Scotia: in addition to the province being referred to as "The Mississippi of the North," references to the American south pop up in *Trailer Park Boys* (for example, when Ricky, Bubbles, and Julian travel to Maine to smuggle drugs, they are terrified about meeting "hillabillies" and finding themselves in a *Deliverance*-type situation), and *a possible madness* is driven by fears of the spread of Mountain Top Removal mining from West Virginia to Cape Breton.

Oxyana, another documentary named for a town whose nickname derives from prescription drugs, also illustrates this connection. Set in Oceana, West Virginia, *Oxyana* is very similar to *Cottonland* in its approach to this subject matter. The documentary explores many of the same themes: the isolation of the community in question, the disconnect between the natural beauty of the setting and the prevalence of drug addiction, and the idea that hillbilly heroin is polluting a long-established way of life. *Oxyana* and *Cottonland* oscillate between interviews with addicts and recovering addicts and interviews with health, social service, and law enforcement officials. One significant difference between the two films is the narrative structure. While *Cottonland* clearly maps the idea of destruction and then rehabilitation on the arc of the film, *Oceana* functions more like a psa on addiction, juxtaposing the faces and bodies of those who are "dirty" (to use an actual phrase from the film) with those who are clean, culminating in the final scenes of the movie with images straight out of the "This is your face on meth" ad campaign as the film cycles through the film's cast of characters, alternating between addict and nonaddict as the credits roll.

Oxyana's approach to the specific subject matter of the film is much more direct and complicated than *Cottonland*. The filmmakers show addicts shooting up numerous times, interviewees talk in specific detail about where they buy their drugs and the ongoing illegal activities they engage in to secure them, and the stories of murder, theft, and personal harm are much more detailed and visceral. One of the interviewees talks about his father killing his mother and brother in a dispute over pills in a very direct and personal way. Elsewhere an interviewee says that she has lost her kids because she is "dirty." The interviews clearly often take place when the subjects are under the influence.

The timeline of decay is also a little harder to pin down in *Oxyana*. Perhaps because the coal-mining industry is more robust in West Virginia, pinpointing the specific moments when things started to fall apart is more difficult. The final stages of the closure of the mines in industrial Cape Breton took place at the end of the 1990s, more or less coinciding with the rise of oxycontin abuse, while the situation in West Virginia is murkier. As in *Cottonland*, the filmmakers focus explicitly on the boundary between nature and culture and dwell throughout the documentary on scenes of nature degraded through various activities, including corporate development (the camera holds several times on 7–Eleven and McDonald's backdropped by the green mountains), industrial development, and the drug use of the inhabitants of Oceana. Mike Moore, a dentist who recently moved to Oceana, talks directly about the disconnect between the beauty of the natural setting and what he sees as the immoral behaviour taking place: "There's this darkness that has come over it that has affected all of those things. I mean, I think in a way it has even affected the natural beauty of this place because as a person that lives here I almost can't look at it the same." Elsewhere, interviewees explicitly connect the shift from the industrial economy to the postindustrial world of service jobs, noting that given the choice between working for minimum wage in retail or at a fast-food restaurant, many young people in rural West Vriginia have opted for selling pills instead.

The documentary also relies on a strict distinction between the rural inhabitants of West Virginia that are its subjects and the assumed urban population that makes up its audience. The film opens with a number of the interviewees shooting guns and driving four-wheelers, and during the course of interviews, subjects often talk directly to the interviewers, asking them things like whether or not they are atheists, telling them they have no idea what it is like to live in such an isolated and hopeless place, and confiding that they would never wish life in Oceana on anyone.

Just as in *Cottonland*, the moral panic surrounding prescription drug abuse seems to be related more to stereotypes and assumptions connected to the drugs and less to the actual tangible effects of them (Young 2017). In the case of Kentucky and West Virginia, Kenneth Tunnell points to the sharp disconnect between media coverage of the epidemic of prescription drug abuse (media coverage focused primarily on experts who referred to skyrocketing incidences of overdoses and violent crimes fuelled by opiate addicts) and reality (in these states, crime rates stayed more or less the same or even dropped during the period immediately following the rise of the "epidemic" in southern Appalachia). Tunnell argues that some of the effects of the drugs (the zombie-like appearance, decaying bodies, propensity toward violence, the amateur nature of their production) and the nicknames of the drugs, particularly hillbilly heroin, fit into pre-existing assumptions and stereotypes about marginal regions such as Appalachia or Atlantic Canada (Tunnell 2004, 137). He argues that drug scares and moral panics have little to do with the reality of what is happening on the ground and are instead connected to the level of rhetoric that surrounds them. In the case of crack and oxycontin addiction, the representations or images we associate with these drugs map easily on to our assumptions about the people who live in the communities most affected by them. Tunnell argues that many of the ideas surrounding these drug epidemics and the moral panic associated with them obscure much more complex issues surrounding these regions, as the stereotypes foisted on to people in the Appalachian or Nova Scotian coalfield constitute a kind of victim-blaming where the people whose landscape and labour were exploited by mineral and timber companies were in turn ravaged by the flight of capital and environmental problems left behind by these industries.

***

In a January 2014 newspaper article published in the *Charleston Gazette-Mail*, Denise Giardina argues that the chemical spill that took place that year in West Virginia's Elk River is an instructive case in the context of North America's response to the prevalence of pollution and drug abuse in places such as Appalachia and Atlantic Canada. Giardina argues that responses to the spill that focused on the idea that West Virginians display "cult-like" behaviour in their willingness to be abused and in "fouling [their] own nest" overlook what she sees as the colonial history of the region (Giardina 2014, 4) – a history that has seen absentee landlords execute power over the natural environment and pollute it with impunity. The discourse surrounding other forms of pollution – prescription drugs, violence, crime, obesity, diabetes – carries with it the same kind of moral stance that obscures the history of resource exploitation, blames the residents of Nova Scotia and West Virginia for the consequences of the industrial era, portrays the societies in question as backward and unable to get their acts together, and assigns blame for the impact of these industrial activities on the people who live in these regions rather than the corporations that undertake them.

The panic over prescription drug abuse in postindustrial Nova Scotia brings together many of the issues I've discussed in this book. Prescription drugs are a byproduct of the industrial era, as doctors overprescribed painkillers to coal miners and other manual labourers; discourses around pollution and contagion fit into other fears about the often invisible things left behind from industrial and extractive activities; this problem speaks to the idea that the working-class body is at risk; and images of prescription drug abuse fuel many of our stereotypes about white trash culture. While there is much popular literature and music from the industrial era about disasters and moments in which bodies explode, burn up, or crumble under mine collapses, the fallout from prescription drugs is slow and is connected to changing patterns of work in less obvious ways. The contemporary literature and popular culture of the region shifts focus to unexpected ways that resource extraction and other industrial activities impact the body, including prescription drugs and the pollution and leftover toxins that form a barely visible but always present part of the physical environment.

6

Conclusion: *What Remains*

Foord Street, Stellarton's main drag, is the heart of Leo McKay's fictional universe. Like McKay, I grew up a few blocks from Foord, and that nondescript road has played an exceedingly important role in my life. My family shopped for groceries there, and it's where I rode my bike, played ball hockey, and went to the library. Every time I return to town after being away for a while, I take a moment to drive down Foord to see what has changed and to take a look at the quirky messages posted on the marquee of the town's shuttered movie theatre.

Perhaps more significantly, Foord Street structures how I think about postindustrial Nova Scotia, as it is a microcosm for the changes and tensions I've described in this book. Named after one of the most significant and dangerous coal seams in Nova Scotia, Foord intersects with a series of other streets named after mine shafts and managers, including Acadia Avenue and Foster Avenue. It is home to the Nova Scotia Museum of Industry, two miners monuments (the public monument across from the cenotaph and the memorial constructed by Sobeys when it opened its head office on Foord in 2000), and it is directly across the East River from the Westray site. In addition to these ever-present and very tangible reminders of the prominence of coal mining in the region's history, Foord is also ground zero for Nova Scotia's service industry, as it houses the entire Sobeys complex, including its head office, its distribution centre, and the company's first grocery store. Foord Street is a living monument to the shift from the industrial era to the postindustrial era and it betrays the complicated connections between the two.

In the fall of 2014, nearly twenty years after the ceremonial destruction of the Westray silos, my wife and I took our two-year-old daughter to the Museum of Industry, a short walk down Foord Street from my parents' house. Hanna, my daughter, spent most of the visit playing in the foyer on the Kid's Train, a brightly coloured locomotive that features, in addition to zoo animals and a slide, a tender where children can shovel pieces of plastic coal. While she was running around, I wandered through a temporary exhibition staged by photographer Eliot Wright and jewellery-maker Liz van Allen (now Liz Wright). Entitled *What Remains: The Nova Scotia Industrial Project*, the exhibition was a striking mix of Wright's Edward Burtynsky-like studies of Nova Scotia's industrial ruins and van Allen's jewellery, both made from and inspired by primary resources such as coal. The exhibition explored many of the themes in this book, including lingering pollution, Nova Scotia's extractive impulse, abandoned space, and the complex feelings of attraction and revulsion inherent in sites like strip mines, slag heaps, and decommissioned factories. Many of the photographs featured industrial ruins, discarded mills and mine shafts, and empty industrial sites. Van Allen captured the sense of eerie romance inherent in these spaces by constructing her pieces from unexpected materials and remnants of the industrial era, including necklaces made from slag and rusted steel.

What Remains took as its starting point the sheer scale of industrial development in Nova Scotia – the unbelievable range of coal shafts, steel foundries, and factories that dotted the province during the nineteenth and twentieth centuries. The photographs and salvage work brought the artists to unexpected places, including into mothballed and deteriorating factories and the bottom of Pioneer's open-pit mine in Stellarton. In searching widely for evidence of the impact of the industrial era on the province's landscape, Wright and van Allen engaged in an act of preservation; bringing exposure to this aspect of the province's history gives visitors a sense of just how advanced Nova Scotia's industrial economy had been. This is a recurring theme in the museum: it is

6.1 Eliot Wright, *Pioneer Coal Mine (II), Stellarton NS, 2013*, from the series *What Remains* (2013–14)

almost unthinkable today that Nova Scotia once had multiple soft drink distributors, ropeworks, textiles factories, and foundries. Wright and van Allen represent deindustrialization as a dramatic process in which these items start disappearing from the landscape and convey the sense that there is an urgent need to find, document, and consume the physical remnants of a time that is quickly fading into distant memory.

Their work clearly plays on the nostalgia and fetishism inherent in our response to resource extraction and industrial development. On the one hand, the juxtaposition of the empty and grown-over industrial sites and the jewellery evokes the romance of the industrial era. At the same time, this material speaks to the impulse to move forward through commemorating this past and through shifting to activities like jewellery and textile-making, which of course are key parts of the region's tourism strategy. Their work combines the banal, everyday grind of industrial work with ostentatious materials designed to be displayed publicly on the body and claims these pieces as examples of the bounty of the industrial

6.2 Eliot Wright, *Nova Forge (I), Trenton* NS, 2013, from the series *What Remains* (2013–14)

era. The presence of the jewellery alongside the photographs of the industrial ruins adds to the sense that these images and the way of life they evoke are strange artifacts from a lost age. The exhibit note also contributes to this feeling: "Increasingly, evidence of our past industrial activity is disappearing from the landscape and so it has never been more important to document it in detail" (Nova Scotia Museum of Industry 2014). The note explicitly refers to the ruins of the industrial era featured in both the photographs and the jewellery as "curiosities" since the way of life they capture has largely disappeared and the physical remains of that way of life are in a process of transformation and decay.

Of course, staging this exhibition in the Museum of Industry had a profound impact on how it was presented. The museum bolstered the exhibition by adding pieces from its collection such

6.3 Liz Wright, *Coal*, from the series *What Remains* (2013–14)

as spools, racks, crucibles, and a foundry pattern. This enhanced the feeling that the exhibition was offering a window into the past and that it was part of a project of preserving (and, in the case of van Allen's jewellery, repurposing) these materials and the traditions surrounding them. The entry for *What Remains* on the Government of Nova Scotia's website speaks directly to this aim and links the exhibition to the narrative of progress and rehabilitation that I've described; one of its sidebars reads, "As we move towards the challenges that lay ahead, we have to ask ourselves: How can we learn from the past to better prepare for our future?" (Government of Nova Scotia 2014).

Ultimately, this phrase gets at the heart of what this book has been about. The official narrative of the shift from the industrial era to the postindustrial era is that this moment took place at a specific time (the end of the 1990s), that it happened discretely and cleanly, that it happened for the right reasons (the industrial era had become dangerous and unsustainable and it was time to move to something more modern and safe), and that the remnants of this era are at once obsolete, salvageable, and even romantic.

6.4 Liz Wright, *Forge*, from the series *What Remains* (2013–14)

This is a story of restoration: the project of the postindustrial era is to sweep away the evidence of what happened before. Representing history in a specific way is a tool for spiritually rehabilitating the region in the same way as parks and recreational spaces physically remediate the landscape. *What Remains* captures this interplay through its focus on the material byproducts of the industrial era presented in a very safe and appealing way, its romantic tone, and its interest in the logic of rehabilitation.

As I've mentioned a number of times in this book, one of the dangers in working with postindustrial landscapes is that they often evoke nostalgic or a-critical responses in both artists and critics. In addition to romanticizing work, the extraction of natural resources, the masculine working-class body, and the social relations these industrial activities engendered, there is a cottage industry for what critical geographers often call "smokestack nostalgia" or "ruin porn." This comes in the form of highly aestheticized coffee table books, calendars, urban exploration websites, and even tours of deindustrialized cities such as Detroit (Cowie and

Heathcott 2003; High and Lewis 2007; Linkon 2013; Strangleman 2013). At the same time, in addition to romanticizing the experience of deindustrialization, artistic representations of these spaces can go in the opposite direction, leading to places such as northern Nova Scotia becoming "identified as sites of failure, decay, and struggle" (Linkon 2013, 38).

The authors and cultural producers I have examined in this book refuse both of these impulses. Their work demonstrates the ambivalent position industrial and extractive activities occupy in northern Nova Scotia's cultural memory and plans for the future. The extraction of natural resources remains particularly important: in addition to the prominence of the industrial heritage complex (and its role in the region's tourism industry), attempts to restart mines in Cape Breton and the movement of workers between the province and the oil sands in Alberta reveal the degree to which these activities and the intellectual framework that sustains them are solidly entrenched in the region. In their provocative book *The Failure of Global Capitalism: From Cape Breton to Colombia and Beyond* (2009), Terry Gibbs and Garry Leech argue that Nova Scotia's existing energy infrastructure – built to be powered by coal – demands that it import coal (even after its own mines have closed) and implicates the province in a global extractive economy that destroys communities and ecosystems and suppresses human rights in places such as Colombia. For them, this system is important in Nova Scotia because of the things left over from the industrial era: Nova Scotia's energy infrastructure is built around being a place with abundant coal, so even in an era where coal-fired plants are shutting down, the province needs to buy coal on the global market in order to keep the lights on.

Gibbs and Leech provide a compelling analysis of the effects of resource extraction, industry, and subsequent deindustrialization on Cape Breton's natural environment and the bodies of the people who live and lived in these communities. The authors reach some challenging conclusions. Ultimately, they maintain that northern Nova Scotia itself is a byproduct of the industrial era and that the community I grew up in and those I wrote about in this book represent a series of problems: they exist, they constitute an ongoing occupation of land originally inhabited by Mi'kmaq communities, and they contest the idea that the region is an abstract space just waiting to be exploited.

This observation also brings into focus the ambivalent response to the industrial and extractive era outlined by the authors and cultural producers I've discussed. Even in *Cottonland*, *Twenty-Six*, *Saints of Big Harbour*, and *a possible madness*, texts that are clearly critical of the human and environmental toll of mining, there is a certain level of reverence for resource extraction and a recognition of the role these activities played in building communities, providing steady work, sustaining social relationships, and establishing the region's infrastructure. It is easy to be nostalgic about all of these things and in a place where there's an impulse to transform everything – culture, the landscape, traditions that may or may not exist, historical moments, even human suffering,[1] in the case of the Museum of Industry – into fodder for the tourism industry, it is unsurprising that these ideas and the narrative of progress they feed into are so prominent.

To return to R.M. Vaughan, this tension is what makes things so complicated in postindustrial Nova Scotia. Seeing the pristine version of Nova Scotia on television commercials and being constantly reminded of the importance of the mining industry to the region's cultural identity has to be frustrating for a generation of people who live in polluted postindustrial landscapes and are weighing the choice between moving to Alberta to find work in the tar sands or staying in Pictou County to work part-time at Sobeys. The literature and popular culture of postindustrial Nova Scotia demonstrates that this story is more complicated than the one crafted by the tourism industry and the state: there are unresolved health and environmental issues, there are polluted and abandoned spaces, there are problematic ideas about gender and ethnicity; and what's more, the destroyed landscape of the region itself has become a key marker of identity and attempts to remediate it serve in part to sanitize the region's history.

Notes

INTRODUCTION

1 In the early 2000s, municipal and provincial governments throughout northern Nova Scotia jostled to attract call centres to the region. Many media stories frame these campaigns in direct connection with the fall of the coal-mining industry, noting that call centres would represent a way to "boost local morale" (Taylor 2000, A11), that these projects would "cushion" the blow of mine closures (McNeil 2002, A3), and noting that officials were even considering the former DEVCO building for a call centre site (Montgomery 2000, 18).

2 This idea also comes up in reconciling Nova Scotia's history of racism. For example, "moving forward" framed much of the official narrative surrounding the Nova Scotia government's granting of a "free pardon" to Viola Desmond in 2010. The lieutenant governor, Mayann Francis, declared that the pardon "close[d] an erroneous chapter in the history of this province and allow[ed] a new one to begin," and then-premier Darrell Dexter described the circumstances surrounding Desmond's arrest and detention as a historical misstep that time would heal, noting, "As we move forward, I want to reaffirm this province's commitment to equality for all Nova Scotians" (Government of Nova Scotia 2010).

3 Key scholarship in Atlantic Canada studies disputes the assumption that the region's twentieth-century downturn was the result of cultural factors and instead locates these issues within a nationalist framework in which Confederation favoured certain regions over others (Alexander 1983; Forbes 1987; McKay 1994; among others).

4 In *Writing the Everyday: Women's Textual Communities in Atlantic Canada* (2004), Danielle Fuller builds on this concept, noting that for

later writers such as Sherrie Fitch and Lynn Coady, the family would become a source of discord and repression (Fuller 2004, 204). As I discuss in the following chapter, Rachel Bryant's *The Homing Place: Indigenous and Settler Literary Legacies of the Atlantic* (2017) addresses the role of the "home place" in the context of settler narratives of belonging in the region.
5 See Calder 1998; Chalykoff 1998; Davey 1997; Hochbruck 1996; MacLeod 2008; among others.
6 See Adams 2005; Campbell 2008; Gordon 2016; Hennessy 2015; Hodd 2008; Ivison 2011; MacDonald 2011; Mannell 2011; Mason 2007; Mason 2013; Morton 2014; Norman 2009; Sparling 2003; Summerby-Murray 2015; Tremblay 2008; Vance 2011; Varga 2015; Wyile 2008; Wyile 2011; Wyile and Lynes 2008.
7 The impact of neoliberalism and late capitalism on the production of culture in Nova Scotia is also the focus of Erin Morton's *For Folk's Sake: Art and Economy in Twentieth-Century Nova Scotia*. In this study, Morton meticulously argues that "folk art in twentieth-century Nova Scotia helped residents of the province reframe the cultural past there in ways that are deeply connected to varying moments of economic, social, and political crisis" (Morton 2016, 300).
8 Many of these images appear on the popular t-shirts and hoodies produced by the Nova Scotia-based clothing company East Coast Lifestyle.
9 Ambivalence toward the specific experience of an industry leaving and a jail appearing has a strong history in Atlantic Canadian literature. For example, this trope is a central part of David Adams Richards's 1984 novel *Road to the Stilt House*. As I discuss in later chapters, incarceration is a key anxiety in contemporary Nova Scotian literature and popular culture: *Blackbird*, *Cottonland*, and *Trailer Park Boys* all connect the province's economic and social conditions to issues surrounding the carceral state.
10 The Northern Pulp paper mill in Pictou has been the site of a wide range of protests and inspired Joan Baxter's *The Mill: Fifty Years of Pulp and Protest* (2017), a book that was so controversial in northern Nova Scotia that a planned book signing had to be cancelled in December of 2017 (Leeder 2017).

CHAPTER ONE

1 Fraser, MacLennan, and MacLeod each refer to the relationship between mining and substance abuse, a theme that is prominent in the

contemporary literature and popular culture of Nova Scotia, including McKay's *Twenty-Six*. As I discuss in chapter 5, the documentary *Cottonland* explores the shift from alcohol to opiates and the impact of this development on the former mining communities of Cape Breton.

2 For more on how this concept plays out in Atlantic Canadian literature, see Rachel Bryant's 2017 study *The Homing Place: Indigenous and Settler Literary Legacies of the Atlantic*, where she argues that through "the shifting idea of the home place, non-Indigenous Maritime writers and readers have articulated, revised, and ultimately controlled their relationships to the places they inhabit, effectively and continuously claiming and imagining this region, to which they are relative newcomers, as their own intellectual property" (Bryant 2017, 4).

3 The pervasive image of moving away from the province takes a number of forms in Nova Scotian literature and popular culture: there are workers who wish to flee the terrible working conditions of the mines, there are ambitious young men and women who see life in industrial Nova Scotia as a trap, and there is the recurring figure of the worker who reluctantly moves away from the region for economic opportunity elsewhere. The latter was dramatized in the 1970 Donald Shebib film *Goin' down the Road*, in which Pete and Joey drive to Toronto to find work. Once there, they are shunned by their relatives and fall on even more economic misfortune. This narrative – found also, for example, in Lynn Coady's "Look, and Pass On" (2000) and Bruce McDonald's *Weirdos* (2016) – establishes a recurring theme in Nova Scotian literature, popular culture, and media: that moving from the province for better fortunes elsewhere is accompanied by either a genuine or an ironic sense of nostalgia for the home place. This ambivalence toward the home place is also very much present in the 1999 film *New Waterford Girl,* where Mooney Pottie dreams of leaving Cape Breton. While the film explores Mooney's frustration with growing up in a small, insular town with an overbearing family, it also ties her desire to leave to New Waterford's relationship with resource extraction. She dismissively tells Lou, her intriguing new neighbour from New York, that the town consists of little more than a mine and a road to Sydney, and she presents "radical" ideas about how the dust and smoke from mining and burning coal is killing everyone in her class, which draws eye-rolls and shock from those present. For more on the "Goin' down the Road" narrative, see Armstrong 2018 and Ramsay 1993.

4 Scenes from "The Return" and "The Boat" (1968) form the basis for Kate Beaton's comic sketch "East Coast Literature."

CHAPTER THREE

1 See Parpart's 1999 essay on *Margaret's Museum*, Ramsay's 1993 essay on *Goin' down the Road*, and Charman's 2018 essay on Alistair MacLeod's short fiction for examples of scholarship on masculinity in Atlantic Canadian literature and popular culture.
2 Of course, this point is debatable: men continue to hold a disproportionate share of power and "control, directly or indirectly, most of the world's resources, capital, media, political parties, and corporations [so it] is difficult to imagine this group in crisis" (Ramsay 2011, xviii).
3 However, Coady complicates this point: every person who meets Gord reports that he is a harmless old man and that Rank is far too hard on him.
4 The novel's opening passages zero in on the relationship between genetics, identity, and self-image. Rank recalls that Adam was "afraid of being fat" (Coady 2011, 3) and that he treated a disposition toward being fat as a "contagion ... the same way ... guys who are actually maybe gay or have the potential for gayness within them" (3).

CHAPTER FOUR

1 As discussed in the previous two chapters, an ambivalent relationship with Scottish symbols is a key part of the work of Coady, McKay, and Campbell.
2 The footloose and romantic version of Scottishness McKay identifies often played down a connection to the urban industrial parts of the province and especially any role in union organizing.
3 There is a strong history of Atlantic Canadian literature that looks to forge an unassailable connection between the region's settler society and the space of North America through narratives of environmental determinism and genetic inheritance (think *Rockbound* [1928], *Galore* [2009], *Gaff Topsails* [1996], *Each Man's Son* [1951], and many others).
4 Of course, this storyline can't help but call to mind the clearing of Africville in the 1960s and the tendency for African-Nova Scotian communities, including Lincolnville, to be adjacent to landfills (Nelson 2008; Perreaux 2010).
5 See Alexander MacLeod's essay, "The Little State of Africadia Is a Community of Believers," (2008), which eloquently examines the

relationship between Clarke's literary work and the political achievements of Africadian nationalism.

6 *When the Saints* includes a familiar feature of much contemporary Nova Scotian literature: recalling how one's father revered *his* father, who inevitably turns out to be essentially the opposite of how he is remembered; in this case, Tabby says that "Daddy talked [Grandpa Jack] up like he was the Messiah when really he was a demented alcoholic tyrant who used to beat Daddy with this black horse statue that sat on the mantle" (12).

7 In Greer's *Tyler's Cape* (2000), Luke learns that his mother crawled down a well in a vain attempt to save his older brother, who had fallen in. She stays in the well for hours with the baby's corpse.

CHAPTER FIVE

1 In 1946, African Nova Scotian businesswoman Viola Desmond was arrested for refusing to sit upstairs in the segregated Roseland Theatre. As I write this, the building is being converted into a restaurant and plans are underway to create space for artwork honouring Desmond in the building.

2 This connection between the fall of the industrial era and the rise of drug use and trafficking is explored in detail in *The Wire*.

3 See, for example, Cronon 1996; Wilson 1991; Haraway 1991; Mazel 2000; Armbruster and Wallace 2001; and Kern 2003.

4 There are countless news stories on this topic; also see documentaries such as Netflix's *Heroin(e)* (2017) and HBO's *Warning: This Drug May Kill You* (2017).

5 The show features several references to Jenna's use of meth.

CHAPTER SIX

1 Describing the failure of Michigan's Autoworld in his 1989 film *Roger and Me*, Michael Moore says, "I guess it was like expecting a million people a year to go to New Jersey to Chemicalworld or a million people going to Valdez, Alaska for Exxonworld. Some people just don't like to celebrate human tragedy while on vacation" (Moore 1989).

Works Cited

A&E Television. 2012–16. *Duck Dynasty*. Los Angeles: Gurney Productions.

Ackerman, Nance. 2006. *Cottonland*. Montreal: NFB Films.

Adams, Annmarie. 2005. "Picturing Vernacular Architecture: Thaddeus Holownia's Photographs of Irving Gas Stations." *Material Culture Review* 61: 36–42.

Alaimo, Stacy. 2010. *Bodily Natures: Science, Environment, and the Material Self*. Bloomington: Indiana University Press.

Alexander, David. 1983. "Canadian Regionalism: A Central Problem." In *Atlantic Canada and Confederation: Essays in Canadian Political Economy*, edited by Eric Sager, Lewis Fischer, and Stuart Pierson, 44–50. Toronto: University of Toronto Press.

Algeo, Katie. 2003. "Locals on Local Color: Imagining Identity in Appalachia." *Southern Cultures* 9 (4): 27–54.

Andreatta, David. 2013. "In Nova Scotia Town, Residents Fight Local Mill's Pollution." *Globe and Mail*, 13 September. http://www.theglobeandmail.com/news/national/in-nova-scotia-town-residents-fight-local-mills-pollution/article14324606/.

Andrews, Thomas. 2008. *Killing for Coal: America's Deadliest Labor War*. Cambridge: Harvard University Press.

Armbruster, Karla, and Kathleen Wallace, eds. 2001. *Beyond Nature Writing: Expanding the Boundaries of Ecocriticism*. Charlottesville: University of Virginia Press.

Armstrong, Christopher. 2010. "The Rock Observed: Art and Surveillance in Michael Winter's *This All Happened*." *Newfoundland and Labrador Studies* 25 (1): 1719–26.

– 2018. "'The Lines We Drive On': Automobility in the Road Narratives of Donald Shebib and Alistair MacLeod." *Studies in Canadian Literature* 43 (2): 40–59.

Armstrong, Christopher, and Herb Wyile. 1997. "Firing the Regional Can(n)on: Liberal Pluralism, Social Agency, and David Adams Richards's Miramichi Trilogy." *Studies in Canadian Literature* 22: 1–18.

Atherton, Stanley. 1984. "Fighting Back: The Regional Renaissance in Recent Canadian Fiction." *World Literature Written in English* 24 (1): 127–34.

Atwood, Margaret. 1972. *Survival: A Thematic Guide to Canadian Literature*. Toronto: Anansi.

Augé, Marc. 1995. *Non-Places: Introduction to an Anthropology of Supermodernity*. Translated by John Howe. London: Verso.

Baxter, Joan. 2017. *The Mill: Fifty Years of Pulp and Protest*. East Lawrencetown: Pottersfield Press.

Beaton, Meaghan, and Del Muise. 2008. "The Canso Causeway, Tartan Tourism, Industrial Development, and the Promise of Progress for Cape Breton." *Acadiensis* 37 (2): 39–69.

Berces, Frances. 1991. "Existential Maritimer: Alistair MacLeod's *The Lost Salt Gift of Blood*." *Studies in Canadian Literature* 16 (1): 114–28.

Bjerre, Thomas. 2012. "Post-9/11 Literary Masculinities in Kalfus, DeLillo, and Hamid." *Orbis Litterarum* 67 (3): 241–66.

Blake, Jason. 2010. *Canadian Hockey Literature: A Thematic Study*. Toronto: University of Toronto Press.

Bluestone, Barry, and Bennett Harrison. 1982. *The Deindustrialization of America: Plant Closings, Community Abandonment, and the Dismantling of Basic Industry*. New York: Basic Books.

Boorman, John. 1972. *Deliverance*. Los Angeles: Warner Bros.

Bruneau, Carol. 1995. *After the Angel Mill*. Dunvegan: Cormorant Books.

Bryant, Rachel. 2017. *The Homing Place: Indigenous and Settler Legacies of the Atlantic*. Waterloo: Wilfrid Laurier University Press.

Buell, Lawrence. 1998. "Toxic Discourse." *Critical Inquiry* 24: 639–65.

Buma, Michael. 2012. *Refereeing Identity: The Cultural Work of Canadian Hockey Novels*. Montreal & Kingston: McGill-Queen's University Press.

Burns, Kevin. 2014–18. *The Curse of Oak Island*. Prometheus Entertainment.

Burns, Shirley Stewart. 2007. *Bringing Down the Mountains: The Impact of Mountaintop Removal Surface Coal Mining on Southern West Virginia Communities, 1970–2004*. Morgantown: West Virginia University Press.

Butler, Judith. 1990. *Gender Trouble: Feminism and the Subversion of Identity*. New York: Routledge.

Buxton, Jason. 2012. *Blackbird*. Toronto: A71 Productions.

Byers, Michele. 2011. "Speaking about the Nation: Critiques from the Canadian Margins." *Critical Studies in Television: The International Journal of Television Studies* 6 (2): 131–53.

Calder, Alison. 1998. "Reassessing Prairie Realism." In *A Sense of Place: Re-evaluating Regionalism in Canadian and American Writing*, edited by Christian Riegel and Herb Wyile, 51–60. Edmonton: University of Alberta Press.

Campbell, Jonathan. 2004. *Tarcadia*. Kentville: Gaspereau Press.

Campbell, Wanda. 2008. "'Every Sea-Surrounded Hour': The Margin in Maritime Poetry." *Studies in Canadian Literature* 33 (2): 151–70.

Canadian Press. 2001. "The Era of Coal Mining in Atlantic Canada Ends." *Daily Mercury*. 24 November. D07.

Cardona, Maria. 2012. "Romney's Empty 'Binders Full of Women.'" CNN, 18 October. http://www.cnn.com/2012/10/17/opinion/cardona-binders-women/

Carroll, Noel. 1987. "The Nature of Horror." *The Journal of Aesthetics and Art Criticism*. 46 (1): 51–9.

Carson, Rachel. 1962. *Silent Spring*. New York: Mahoney and Rose.

CBC News. 2003. "More 'Hillbilly Heroin' in Cape Breton." *CBC News Nova Scotia,* 22 May. http://www.cbc.ca/news/canada/nova-scotia/more-hillbilly-heroin-in-cape-breton-1.370835.

– 2010. "New Jail to Be Built in Pictou County." 1 November. https://www.cbc.ca/news/canada/nova-scotia/new-jail-to-be-built-in-pictou-county-1.956489.

Chafe, Paul. 2008. "Beautiful Losers: The Flâneur in St John's Literature." *Newfoundland and Labrador Studies* 23 (2): 116–38.

Chalykoff, Lisa. 1998. "Overcoming the Two Solitudes of Canadian Literary Regionalism." *Studies in Canadian Literature* 23 (1): 160–77.

– 2000. "Space and Identity Formation in Twentieth-Century Canadian Realist Novels: Recasting Regionalism in Canadian Literary Studies." PhD dissertation, University of British Columbia.

Charman, Caitlin. 2018. "'It seems to bust your balls': Coal Nostalgia, Masculinity, and Energy History in Alistair MacLeod's Short Fiction." *Studies in Canadian Literature* 43 (2): 60–78.

Chopra-Gant, Mike. 2012. "'You want me to lick your balls, Daddy?': Masculinity, Race, and Power in *The Shield*." In *Interrogating The Shield*, edited by Nicholas Ray, 124–44. Syracuse: Syracuse University Press.

Clark, Joan. 1994. "God's Country." In *An Underlying Reverence: Stories from Cape Breton*, edited by James Taylor, 73–85. Sydney: UCCB Press.

Clarke, Amy. 2014. "Translating Scottishness from the Homeland to the Diaspora: A Consideration of Nova Scotia's 'Scottish' Architectural Landscape." In *Proceedings of the Society of Architectural Historians, Australia and New Zealand*, edited by Christoph Schnoor, 39–49. Queensland: SAHANZ.

Clattenburg, Mike. 2001–. *Trailer Park Boys*. Halifax: Trailer Park Productions.

Clattenburg, Mike, et al. 1999. *Pit Pony*. Cochran Entertainment.

Coady, Lynn. 1998. *Strange Heaven*. Fredericton: Goose Lane Editions.

– 2000. *Play the Monster Blind*. Toronto: Doubleday Canada.

– 2002. *Saints of Big Harbour*. Toronto: Doubleday Canada.

– 2003. "Books That Say Arse." In *Victory Meat: New Fiction from Atlantic Canada*, edited by Lynn Coady, 1–6. Toronto: Doubleday Canada.

– 2006. *Mean Boy*. Toronto: Doubleday Canada.

– 2011. *The Antagonist*. Toronto: House of Anansi.

– 2013. "The Twilight of the Patriarchs: Don't Expect Them to Go Quietly." *Eighteen Bridges*, 27 May. http://eighteenbridges.com/story/twilight-patriarchs-rush-limbaugh/.

Cogswell, Fred. 1985. "Some Notes on the Development of Regional Fiction in the Maritimes." *Essays on Canadian Writing* 31: 192–200.

Coleman, Daniel. 2008. *White Civility: The Literary Project of English Canada*. Toronto: University of Toronto Press.

Connell, R.W. 1995. *Masculinities*. Berkeley: University of California Press.

Cowan, Paul. 2001. *Westray*. Montreal: National Film Board.

Cowie, Jefferson, and Joseph Heathcott, eds. 2003. *Beyond the Ruins: The Meanings of Deindustrialization*. Ithaca: ILR Press.

Creelman, David. 2003. *Setting in the East: Maritime Realist Fiction*. Montreal & Kingston: McGill-Queen's University Press.

Cronon, William. 1996. "The Trouble with Wilderness: or, Getting Back to the Wrong Nature." In *Uncommon Ground: Rethinking the Human Place in Nature*, edited by William Cronon, 69–90. New York: Norton.

Crummey, Michael. 2009. *Galore*. Toronto: Doubleday Canada.

Currie, Sheldon. 1995. *The Glace Bay Miners' Museum: The Novel*. Wreck Cove: Breton Books.

Daigle, Bethany. 2018. "Spectres of Pictou County: Regional Hauntings in Leo McKay Jr's *Twenty-Six*." *Studies in Canadian Literature* 43 (2): 167–87.

Davey, Frank. 1997. "Toward the Ends of Regionalism." In *A Sense of Place: Re- evaluating Regionalism in Canadian and American Writing*, edited by Christian Riegel and Herb Wyile, 1–17. Edmonton: University of Alberta Press.

Davies, Gwendolyn, ed. 1991. *Studies in Maritime Literary History, 1760–1930*. Fredericton: Acadiensis Press.

– ed. 1993. *Myth and Milieu: Atlantic Literature and Culture 1918–1939*. Fredericton: Acadiensis Press.

Day, Frank Parker. 1928. *Rockbound*. Toronto: University of Toronto Press.

DeFino, Dean. 2009. "From Trailer Trash to *Trailer Park Boys*." *Post Script* 28 (3): 47–57.

Deitering, Cynthia. 1996. "The Postnatural Novel: Toxic Consciousness in Fiction of the 1980s." In *The Ecocriticism Reader: Landmarks in Literary Ecology*, edited by Cheryll Glotfelty and Harold Fromm, 196–203. Athens: University of Georgia Press.

Delisle, Jennifer Bowering. 2013. *The Newfoundland Diaspora: Mapping the Literature of Outmigration*. Waterloo: Wilfrid Laurier University Press.

Deneault, Alain, and William Sacher. 2012. *Imperial Canada Inc.: Legal Haven of Choice for the World's Mining Industries*. Translated by Fred A. Reed and Robin Philpot. Vancouver: Talonbooks.

Dunk, Thomas. 2003. *It's a Working Man's Town: Male Working-Class Culture*. Montreal & Kingston: McGill-Queen's University Press.

Dunkley, Ria, Nigel Morgan, and Sheena Westwood. 2011. "Visiting the Trenches: Exploring Meanings and Motivations in Battlefield Tourism." *Tourism Management* 32: 860–8.

Dunne, Sean. 2013. *Oxyana*. White Plains: Cadillac Hash.

Edensor, Tim. 2005. *Industrial Ruins: Spaces, Aesthetics and Materiality*. New York: Berg.

Edwards, J. Arwel, and Joan Carles Llurdés I Coit. 1996. "Mines and Quarries: Industrial Heritage Tourism." *Annals of Tourism Research* 23 (2): 341–63.

Edwards, Tim. 2006. *Cultures of Masculinity*. New York: Routledge.

Falkof, Nicky. 2012. "The Father, the Failure, and the Self-Made Man: Masculinity in *Mad Men*." *Critical Quarterly* 54 (3): 31–45.

Ferguson, Michelle. 2013. *Why Here?* Ottawa: Borealis Press.

Fey, Tina. 2006–13. *30 Rock*. New York: Broadway Video.

Fleras, Augie, and Shane Dixon. 2011. "Cutting, Driving, Digging, and Harvesting: Re-masculinizing the Working-Class Heroic." *Canadian Journal of Communication* 36 (4): 579–97.

Forbes, Ernest. 1987. *Challenging the Regional Stereotype*. Fredericton: Acadiensis Press.

Frank, David, and Don MacGillivray. 1992. "Introduction: Dawn Fraser and Cape Breton." In *Echoes from Labor's Wars*, edited by David Frank and Don MacGillivray. Wreck Cove: Breton Books.

Frank, David, Don MacGillivray, and Nicole Lang. 2010. *Labour Landmarks in New Brunswick*. Edmonton: Canadian Committee on Labour History.

Fraser, Dawn. 1992. *Echoes from Labor's Wars*, edited by David Frank and Don MacGillivray. Wreck Cove: Breton Books.

Frye, Northrop. 1971. *The Bush Garden*. Toronto: Anansi.

Fuller, Danielle. 2004. *Writing the Everyday: Women's Textual Communities in Atlantic Canada*. Montreal & Kingston: McGill-Queen's University Press.

Giardina, Denise. 2014. "Harrop Chose Wrong Word for W.Va." *Charleston Gazette-Mail*, 24 January. http://www.wvgazettemail.com/Opinion/201401240143.

Gibbs, Terry, and Garry Leech. 2009. *The Failure of Global Capitalism: From Cape Breton to Colombia and Beyond*. Sydney: Cape Breton University Press.

Gilligan, Vince. 2008–13. *Breaking Bad*. Los Angeles: Sony Pictures Television.

Goodkind, Nicole. 2018. "Did Trump End the War on Clean Coal? Fact-Checking the President's State of the Union Claim." *Newsweek*. 1 January. https://www.newsweek.com/clean-coal-energy-state-union-fact-check-795749.

Gordon, Alan. 2016. *Time Travel: Tourism and the Rise of the Living History Museum in Mid-Twentieth-Century Canada*. Vancouver: UBC Press.

Government of Nova Scotia. 2010. "Late Viola Desmond Granted Apology, Free Pardon." Government of Nova Scotia Website. 15 April. http://novascotia.ca/news/smr/2010-04-15-pardon.asp

– 2014. *What Remains: The Nova Scotia Industrial Project*. Government of Nova Scotia Website. https://museumofindustry.novascotia.ca/what-see-do/feature-exhibit/what-remains-nova-scotia-industrial-project.

Greer, Darren. 2000. *Tyler's Cape*. Toronto: Cormorant Books.

– 2014. *Just beneath My Skin*. Toronto: Cormorant Books.

Guilford, Irene, ed. 2001. *Alistair MacLeod: Essays on His Works*. Toronto: Guernica.

Hage, Ghassan. 2011. "Cultures of Extraction." 21st Century Blog. http://21cblog.com/cultures-of-extraction-by-ghassan-hage/.

Haraway, Donna. 1991. *Simians, Cyborgs and Women: The Reinvention of Nature*. New York: Routledge.

Hartigan, John. 1997. "Unpopular Culture: The Case of 'White Trash.'" *Cultural Studies* 11 (2): 316–43.

– 2005. *Odd Tribes: Toward a Cultural Analysis of White People*. Durham: Duke University Press.

Harvie, Debbi. 2014a. "Attacker Gets 10 Years in Prison." *Pictou Advocate*, 18 June. http://www.pictouadvocate.com/2014/06/18/attacker-gets-10-years-in-prison/.

– 2014b. "Closing Statements Given in Falconer Murder Trial." *Pictou Advocate*, 24 January. http://www.pictouadvocate.com/2014/01/24/closing-statements-given-in-falconer-murder-trial/.

Heise, Ursula. 2002. "Toxins, Drugs, and Global Systems: Risk and Narrative in the Contemporary Novel." *American Literature* 74 (4): 748–78.

Hennessy, Jeffrey J. 2015. "Deterritorialization and Reterritorialization in Atlantic Canadian Popular Music." *MUSICultures* 42 (1): 66–88.

High, Steven, and David Lewis. 2007. *Corporate Wasteland: The Landscape and Memory of Deindustrialization*. Ithaca: ILR Press.

Hiscock, Andrew. 2000. "'This Inherited Life': Alistair MacLeod and the Ends of History." *Journal of Commonwealth Literature* 35 (2): 51–70.

Hochbruck, Wolfgang. 1996. "Centre and Margin: Literature from the Maritimes." In *Down East: Critical Essays on Contemporary Maritime Canadian Literature*, edited by Wolfgang Hochbruck and James Taylor, 9–22. Trier: Wissenschaftlicher Verlag Trier.

Hodd, Thomas. 2008. "Shoring against Our Ruin: Sheldon Currie, Alistair MacLeod, and the Heritage Preservation Narrative." *Studies in Canadian Literature* 33 (2): 191–209.

Hodgins, Peter, and Peter Thompson. 2011. "Taking the Romance out of Extraction: Contemporary Canadian Artists and the Subversion of the Romantic/Extractive Gaze." *Environmental Communication: A Journal of Nature and Culture* 5 (4): 393–410.

Horrocks, Roger. 1995. *Male Myths and Icons: Masculinity in Popular Culture*. London: Macmillan.

Hughes-Fuller, Patricia. 2009. "Wild Bodies and True Lies: Carnival, Spectacle, and the Curious Case of *Trailer Park Boys*." *Canadian Journal of Communication* 34: 95–109.

Hynes, Joel Thomas. 2018 –. *Little Dog*. Toronto: CBC Television Co.

Ivison, Douglas. 2011. "'It's no different than anywhere else': Regionalism, Place, and Popular Culture in Lynn Coady's *Saints of Big Harbour*." *Canadian Literature* 208: 109–25.

Jacobson, Matthew. 1998. *Whiteness of a Different Color: European Immigrants and the Alchemy of Race*. Cambridge: Harvard University Press.

Jarraway, David. 2012. "'Becoming-Woman': Masculine 'Emergency' after 9/11 in Cormac McCarthy." *Canadian Review of American Studies* 42 (1): 49–64.

Jiwani, Yasmin. 2006. "Framing Culture, Talking Race" In *Canadian Cultural Poesis*, edited by Garry Sherbert, Annie Gerin, and Sheila Petty, 99–115. Waterloo: Wilfrid Laurier University Press.

Jobb, Dean. 1994. *Calculated Risk: Greed, Politics, and the Westray Tragedy*. Halifax: Nimbus Publishing.

Kavanagh, Patrick. 1996. *Gaff Topsails*. Dunvegan: Cormorant Books.

Kern, Robert. 2003. "Ecocriticism: What Is It Good For?" In *The Isle Reader*, edited by Michael Branch and Scott Slovic, 258–81. Athens: University of Georgia Press.

Kotcheff, Ted. 1989. *Weekend at Bernie's*. Los Angeles: Gladden Entertainment.

Kulyk Keefer, Janice. 1987. *Under Eastern Eyes: A Critical Reading of Maritime Fiction*. Toronto: University of Toronto Press.

Laghi, Brian. 2002. "Premiers Tell Harper His Attack Was Wrong." *Globe and Mail*, 30 May. https://www.theglobeandmail.com/news/national/premiers-tell-harper-his-attack-was-wrong/article4135715/.

Lee, Ruthann. 2011. "The Production of Racialized Masculinities in Contemporary North American Popular Culture." PhD dissertation, York University.

Leeder, Jessica. 2017. "Pulp Non-Fiction: Why a Book about a Nova Scotia Pulp Mill Has Set off a Firestorm." *Globe and Mail*, 6 December. https://www.theglobeandmail.com/news/national/pulp-non-fiction-debate-roils-nova-scotia-town/article37232016/.

Lemky, Kim, and Lee Jolliffe. 2011. "Mining Heritage and Tourism in the Former Coal Mining Communities of Cape Breton Island, Canada." In *Mining Heritage and Tourism: A Global Synthesis*, edited by Michael V. Conlin and Lee Jolliffe, 144–57. London: Routledge.

Linkon, Sherry Lee. 2013. "Narrating the Past and Future: Deindustrialized Landscapes as Resources." *International Labor and Working Class History* 84: 38–54.

Linnemann, Travis, and Tyler Wall. 2013. "'This is your face on meth': The Punitive Spectacle of 'White Trash' in the Rural War on Drugs." *Theoretical Criminology* 17 (3): 315–34.

Little, J.I. 2015. "'A Fine, Hardy, Good-Looking Race of People': Travel Writers, Tourism Promoters, and the Highland Scots Identity on Cape Breton Island, 1829–1920." *Acadiensis* 44 (1): 20–35.

Lochhead, Douglas. 1985. "Atlantic Regionalism and Literature: Some Bibliographical Comments." *Essays on Canadian Writing* 31: 262–6.

MacDonald, Edward. 2011. "A Landscape ... with Figures: Tourism and Environment on Prince Edward Island." *Acadiensis* 40 (1): 70–85.

Macdonald, Frank. 2011. *a possible madness*. Sydney: Cape Breton University Press.

MacDougall, Angus. 1994. "An Underlying Reverence." In *An Underlying Reverence: Stories from Cape Breton*, edited by James Taylor, 49–62. Sydney: UCCB Press.

MacInnes, John. 1998. *The End of Masculinity: The Confusion of Sexual Genesis and Sexual Difference in Modern Society*. Philadelphia: Open University Press.

Mackey, Eva. 2000. "Death by Landscape: Race, Nature and Gender in Nationalist Mythology." *Canadian Women's Studies* 20 (2): 125–30.

– 2002. *The House of Difference: Cultural Politics and National Identity in Canada*. Toronto: University of Toronto Press.

MacKinnon, Lachlan. 2013a. "Labour and the Commemorative Landscape in Industrial Cape Breton, 1922–2013." *Material Culture Review* 77/78: 56–75.

– 2013b "Labour Landmarks in New Waterford: Collective Memory in a Cape Breton Coal Town." *Acadiensis* 42 (2): 3–25.

MacKinnon, Richard. 2008. "Protest Song and Verse in Cape Breton Island." *Ethnologies* 30 (2): 33–71.

MacLennan, Hugh. 1951. *Each Man's Son*. Toronto: Stoddart Publishing.

MacLeod, Alexander. 2008. "'The Little State of Africadia Is a Community of Believers': Replacing the Regional and Remaking the Real in the Work of George Elliott Clarke." *Studies in Canadian Literature* 33 (2): 96–114.

MacLeod, Alistair. 2000. *Island*. Toronto: McClelland and Stewart.

– 2003. *No Great Mischief*. Toronto: McLelland and Stewart.

Mannell, Steven. 2011. "The Dream (and Lie) of Progress: Modern Heritage, Regionalism, and Folk Traditions in Atlantic Canada." *JSSAC/JSÉAC* 36 (1): 93–105.

Marshall, Susanne. 2008. "'As if there were just the two choices': Region and Cosmopolis in Lisa Moore's Short Fiction." *Studies in Canadian Literature* 33 (2): 80–95.

Mason, Courtney. 2007. "The Glengarry Highland Games, 1948–2003: Problematizing the Role of Tourism, Scottish Cultural Institutions, and the Cultivation of Nostalgia in the Construction of Identities." *International Journal of Canadian Studies* 35: 13–38.

Mason, Jody. 2013. "A Family of Migrant Workers: Region and the Rise of Neoliberalism in the Fiction of Alistair MacLeod." *Studies in Canadian Literature* 38 (1): 151–69.

Mathews, Lawrence. 2004. "Report from the Country of No Country." *Essays on Canadian Writing* 82: 1–20.

Mazel, David. 2000. *American Literary Environmentalism*. Athens: University of Georgia Press.

McCullough, John. 2009. "Imperialism, Regionalism, Humanism: *Gullage's*, *Trailer Park Boys*, and Representations of Canadian Space in Global Hollywood." In *Rain/Drizzle/Fog: Film and Television in*

Atlantic Canada, edited by Darrell Varga, 151–70. Calgary: University of Calgary Press.

McDonald, Bruce. 2016. *Weirdos*. Halifax: Holdfast Pictures.

McGregor, Gaile. 1985. *The Wacousta Syndrome: Explorations in the Canadian Langscape*. Toronto: University of Toronto Press.

McKay, Ian. 1992. "Tartanism Triumphant: The Construction of Scottishness in Nova Scotia, 1933–1954." *Acadiensis* 21 (2): 5–47.

– 1994. *The Quest of the Folk: Antimodernism and Cultural Selection in Twentieth-Century Nova Scotia*. Montreal & Kingston: McGill-Queen's University Press.

McKay, Ian, and Robin Bates. 2010. *In the Province of History: The Making of the Public Past in Twentieth-Century Nova Scotia*. Montreal & Kingston: McGill-Queen's University Press.

McKay, Ian, and Jamie Swift. 2012. *Warrior Nation: Rebranding Canada in an Age of Anxiety*. Toronto: Between the Lines.

McKay, Leo. 1995. *Like This: Stories*. Concord: Anansi.

– 2003. *Twenty-Six*. Toronto: McLelland & Stewart.

McNeil, Greg. 2002. "Call Centre Cushions Blow of Coal Mine Closures." *Cape Breton Post*, 24 December. A3.

McMillion Sheldon, Elaine. 2017. *Heroin(e)*. Netflix.

Medovarski, Andrea. 2011. "'Boxing ain't no game': Clement Virgo's *Poor Boy's Game* as Canadian Racial Counter-narrative." *Topia* 22: 117–37.

Messner, Michael. 1992. *Power at Play: Sports and the Problem of Masculinity*. Boston: Beacon Press.

Mian, Sarah. 2015. *When the Saints*. Toronto: HarperCollins Canada.

Mirabello, Doug. 2012–14. *Here Comes Honey Boo Boo*. Burbank: Authentic Entertainment.

Montgomery, Sharon. 2000. "Call Centre Officials Eyeing DEVCO Building." *Cape Breton Post*. 1 November. 18.

Moore, Michael. 1989. *Roger and Me*. Burbank: Warner Brothers.

Morton, Erin. 2014. "Not a Vacation, but a Hardening Process: The Self-Empowerment Work of Therapeutic Craft in Nova Scotia." *Culture Unbound* 6: 773–89.

– 2016. *For Folk's Sake: Art and Economy in Twentieth-Century Nova Scotia*. Montreal & Kingston: McGill-Queen's University Press.

Morton, Timothy. 2007. *Ecology without Nature: Rethinking Environmental Aesthetics*. Cambridge: Harvard University Press.

Moyle, Alan. 1999. *New Waterford Girl*. Toronto: Sienna Films.

Muise, Del. 1998. "Who Owns History Anyway? Reinventing Atlantic Canada for Pleasure and Profit." *Acadiensis* 27 (2): 124–34.

Nelson, Jennifer. 2008. *Razing Africville: A Geography of Racism.* Toronto: University of Toronto Press.

Nitzberg, Julien. 2009. *The Wild and Wonderful Whites of West Virginia.* New York: MTV Studios.

Nixon, Rob. 2011. *Slow Violence and the Environmentalism of the Poor.* Cambridge: Harvard University Press.

Norgaard, K.M. 1999. "Moon Phases, Menstrual Cycles, and Mother Earth: The Construction of a Special Relationship between Women and Nature." *Ethics and the Environment* 4 (2): 197–209.

Norman, Alison. 2009. "'A highly favoured people': The Planter Narrative and the 1928 Grand Historic Pageant of Kentville, Nova Scotia." *Acadiensis* 38 (2): 116–40.

Nova Scotia Museum of Industry. 2014. *What Remains: The Nova Scotia Industrial Project.* The Nova Scotia Museum Website. https://museumofindustry.novascotia.ca/what-see-do/feature-exhibit/what-remains-nova-scotia-industrial-project.

O'Connell, Anne. 2010. "An Exploration of Redneck Whiteness in Multicultural Canada." *Social Politics: International Studies in Gender, State and Society* 17 (4): 536–63.

O'Donnell, John C., ed. 1975. *The Men of the Deeps.* Waterloo: Waterloo Music Company.

Overton, James. 1996. *Making a World of Difference: Essays on Tourism, Culture, and Development in Newfoundland.* St John's: ISER Books.

Parpart, Lee. 1999. "Pit(iful) Male Bodies: Colonial Masculinity, Class and Folk Innocence in *Margaret's Museum.*" *Canadian Journal of Film Studies* 8 (1): 63–86.

Peltz, Perri. 2018. *Warning: This Drug May Kill You.* HBO.

Perreaux, Les. 2010. "Racism's Long History in Quiet East Coast Towns." *Globe and Mail,* 21 May. www.theglobeandmail.com/news/national/racisms-long-history-in-quiet-east-coast-towns/article1241300/?page=all.

Pezzullo, Phaedra. 2007. *Toxic Tourism: Rhetorics of Pollution, Travel, and Environmental Justice.* Tuscaloosa: University of Alabama Press.

Ramsay, Christine. 1993. "Canadian Narrative Cinema from the Margins: 'The Nation' and Masculinity in *Goin' down the Road.*" *Canadian Journal of Film Studies* 2 (2–3): 27–50.

– 2011. *Making It Like a Man: Canadian Masculinities in Practice.* Waterloo: Wilfrid Laurier University Press.

Razack, Sherene. 2002. *Race, Space, and the Law.* Toronto: Between the Lines.

Renan, Ernest. 1990. "What Is a Nation?" In *Nation and Narration*, edited by Homi Bhabha, 8–22. New York: Routledge.

Richer, Shawna. 2003. "'Hillbilly Heroin Hits Cape Breton." *Globe and Mail*, 10 March. http://www.theglobeandmail.com/news/national/hillbilly-heroin-hits-cape-breton/article4127611/.

Robinson, Sally. 2000. *Marked Men: White Masculinity in Crisis.* New York: Columbia University Press.

Ryan, Shawn. 2002–08. *The Shield.* Los Angeles: Sony Pictures Television.

Sandilands, Catriona. 1997. "Mother Earth, the Cyborg, and the Queer: Ecofeminism and (More) Questions of Identity." *NWSA Journal* 9 (3): 18–40.

– 2011. "Cap Rouge Remembered? Whiteness, Scenery, and Memory in Cape Breton Highlands National Park." In *Rethinking the Great White North: Race, Nature, and the Historical Geographies of Whiteness in Canada*, edited by Andrew Baldwin, Laura Cameron, and Audrey Kobayashi, 62–84. Vancouver: UBC Press.

Scott, Rebecca. 2010. *Removing Mountains: Extracting Nature and Identity in the Appalachian Coalfields.* Minneapolis: University of Minnesota Press.

Seaman, Andrew. 1976. "Fiction in Atlantic Canada." *Canadian Literature* 68/9: 26–39.

Shebib, Donald. 1970. *Goin' down the Road.* Toronto: Evdon Films.

Simon, David. 2002–08. *The Wire.* Los Angeles: Home Box Office.

Sparling, Heather. 2003. "'Music Is Language and Language Is Music': Language Attitudes and Musical Choices in Cape Breton, Nova Scotia." *Ethnologies* 25 (2): 145–71.

Stone, Philip, and Richard Sharpley. 2008. "Consuming Dark Tourism: A Thanatological Perspective." *Annals of Tourism Research* 35 (2): 574–95.

Strangleman, Tim. 2013. "'Smokestack Nostalgia,' 'Ruin Porn' or Working-Class Obituary: The Role and Meaning of Deindustrial Representation." *International Labor and Working Class History* 84: 23–37.

Sugars, Cynthia. 2008. "Repetition with a Difference: The Paradox of Origins in Alistair MacLeod's *No Great Mischief.*" *Studies in Canadian Literature* 33 (2): 133–50.

– ed. 2004. *Unhomely States: Theorizing English-Canadian Postcolonialism*. Peterborough: Broadview.

Summerby-Murray, Robert. 2015. "Regenerating Cultural Identity through Industrial Heritage Tourism: Visitor Attitudes, Entertainment and the Search for Authenticity at Mills, Mines and Museums of Maritime Canada." *London Journal of Canadian Studies* 30 (1): 64–89.

Sweeney, Gael. 2001. "The Trashing of White Trash: *Natural Born Killers* and the Appropriation of the White Trash Aesthetic." *Quarterly Review of Film and Video* 18 (2): 43–155.

Taylor, James. 1996. "Celtic Themes and the Comic in Sheldon Currie's 'The Glace Bay Miners' Museum.'" In *Down East: Critical Essays on Contemporary Maritime Canadian Literature*, edited by Wolfgang Hochbruck and James Taylor, 145–56. Trier: Wissenschaftlicher Verlag Trier.

Taylor, Peter. 2000. "Cape Breton Looks at Spending Its Last $80m in Government Money for DEVCO; Some Favour a Call Centre." *National Post*. 23 March. A11.

The News. 2013. "Record Bath Salts Bust in Pictou County." 25 January. http://www.ngnews.ca/News/Local/2013-01-25/article-3163573/Record-bath-salts-bust-in-Pictou-County/1.

Theriault, Vernon. 2019. *Westray: My Journey from Darkness to Light*. Halifax: Nimbus Publishing.

Tremblay, Tony. 2008. "'Lest on too close sight I miss the darling illusion': The Politics of the Centre in 'Reading Maritime.'" *Studies in Canadian Literature* 33 (2): 23–39.

Tunbridge, J.E., and Gregory Ashworth. 1996. *Dissonant Heritage: The Management of the Past as a Resource in Conflict*. New York: J. Wiley.

Tunnell, Kenneth. 2004. "Cultural Constructions of the Hillbilly Heroin and Crime Problem." In *Cultural Criminology Unleashed*, edited by Jeff Ferrell, Keith Hayward, Wayne Morrison, and Mike Presdee, 133–42. London: Glass House.

Twohig, Peter, and Colin Howell. 2009. "A Region on Film: Metropolitanism, Place, and Meaning in NFB Films." In *Rain/Drizzle/Fog: Film and Television in Atlantic Canada*, edited by Darrell Varga, 1–23. Calgary: University of Calgary Press.

Urry, John. 2002. *The Tourist Gaze*. London: Sage.

Vance, Michael. 2011. "From Cape Breton to Vancouver Island: Studying the Scots in Canada." *Immigrants and Minorities* 29 (2): 175–94.

Varga, Darrell. 2015. *Shooting from the East: Filmmaking on the Canadian Atlantic*. Montreal & Kingston: McGill-Queen's University Press.

Vaughan, R.M. 1994. "Lobster Is King: Infantilizing Maritime Culture." *Semiotext(e)* 6 (2): 169–72.

Virgo, Clement. 2007. *Poor Boy's Game*. Halifax: Astral Media.

Walby, Kevin, and Justin Piché. 2011. "The Polysemy of Punishment Memorialization: Dark Tourism and Ontario's Penal History Museums." *Punishment and Society* 13 (4): 451–72.

Wiebe, Sarah. 2010. "Bodies on the Line: The In/Security of Everyday Life in Aamjiwnaang." *New Issues in Security* 5: 1–17.

Williams, David. 2001. "From Clan to Nation." In *Alistair MacLeod: Essays on His Works*, edited by Irene Guilford, 43–71. Toronto: Guernica.

Williams, Raymond. 1980. *Problems in Materialism and Culture: Selected Essays*. London: Verso.

Wilson, Alexander. 1991. *The Culture of Nature: North American Landscape from Disney to the Exxon Valdez*. Toronto: Between the Lines.

Wilz, Kelly. 2016. "Bernie Bros and Woman Cards: Rhetorics of Sexism, Misogyny, and Constructed Masculinity in the 2016 Election." *Women's Studies in Communication* 39 (4): 357–60.

Workman, Thom. 2003. *Social Torment: Globalization in Atlantic Canada*. Halifax: Fernwood.

Wray, Matt. 2006. *Not Quite White: White Trash and the Boundaries of Whiteness*. Durham: Duke University Press.

Wray, Matt, and Annalee Newitz. 1997. *White Trash: Race and Class in America*. New York: Routledge.

Wyile, Herb. 2006. "As for Me and Me Arse: Strategic Regionalism and the Home Place in Lynn Coady's *Strange Heaven*." *Canadian Literature* 189: 85–101.

– 2008. "Going out of Their Way: Tourism, Authenticity, and Resistance in Contemporary Atlantic Canadian Literature." *English Studies in Canada* 34 (2–3): 159–80.

– 2011. *Anne of Tim Hortons: Globalization and the Reshaping of Atlantic-Canadian Literature*. Waterloo: Wilfrid Laurier University Press.

Wyile, Herb, and Jeanette Lynes. 2008. "Surf's Up: The Rising Tide of Atlantic-Canadian Literature." *Studies in Canadian Literature* 33 (2): 5–22.

Young, Stephen. 2017. "Wild, Wonderful, White Criminality: Images of 'White Trash' Appalachia." *Critical Criminology* 25 (1): 103–17.

Index

Acadians, 21, 23, 48, 93–4, 96, 98; in *Saints of Big Harbour*, 80–3
African Nova Scotians, 94, 103–7
After the Angel Mill, 44–6. *See also* Bruneau, Carol
Alaimo, Stacy, 121–2
Antagonist, The, 84–8; adoption in, 86; class in, 84–5; male anxieties in, 84–8; social media in, 87–8. *See also* Coady, Lynn
Appalachia, 16, 24, 28, 51, 120, 124, 130, 134–6

Baxter, Joan, 146n10
Beaton, Kate, 41, 147n4
Blackbird, 88–90. *See also* Buxton, Jason
Boat Harbour, 16–17
Bowles, Corey, 105
boxing, 35, 77–8, 83, 105–7
Bruneau, Carol, 44–6; *After the Angel Mill*, 44–6
Bryant, Rachel, 146n4, 147n2
Bush, George W., 75
Buxton, Jason, 88–90; *Blackbird*, 88–90

call centres, 3, 6–7, 19, 49, 54, 101, 145n1
Campbell, Jonathan, 61–5, 67; *Tarcadia*, 61–5
Cape Breton, 7–8, 17, 24, 45, 48, 121–5, 130–3, 143; Canso Causeway, 22, 39, 48, 95–6; Cape Breton Development Corporation, 6–7, 145n1; Cape Breton Highlands National Park, 48, 96–7; Cape Breton Miners' Museum, 6, 49–50, 52–5; in Coady's fiction, 23, 76–88, 93–4; coal mining in, 6, 8, 15, 27, 69, 143; in Fraser's poetry, 26–33; in MacLennan's fiction, 33–8; in Macleod's fiction, 38–42; oral tradition in, 29; Scottish culture in, 33–4, 43–4, 61–2, 67–8, 83, 93, 95–100, 116; Sydney Steel Corporation, 6–7; in *Tarcadia*, 61–5
Clark, Joan, 26, 44–5
Clarke, George Elliott, 104, 107, 149n5
Coady, Lynn, 6, 23, 38, 70–90, 93–4, 111–12, 117, 126,

146n4; *The Antagonist*, 84–8;
"Play the Monster Blind,"
77–80; *Saints of Big Harbour*,
79–83, 93–4 144; *Strange
Heaven*, 71, 79, 126
coal mining, 3, 6–8, 15, 18–19,
22, 42–6, 76, 90, 137–43; in
Cottonland and *Oxyana*, 129–
35; effects on the body, 50;
in Fraser's poetry, 26–33; in
MacLennan's fiction, 33–8;
in MacLeod's fiction, 40–2;
memorialization of, 25–9,
50–5; and nostalgia, 113; in
a possible madness, 65–8;
and Scottish culture, 95–6;
in *Twenty-Six*, 55–61; and
war imagery, 27–8, 58
Connell, R.W., 74–5
Cottonland, 24, 120–21, 129–35,
144, 147n1
Creelman, David, 12–13
Currie, Sheldon, 42–3, 98–9
Curse of Oak Island, The, 15–16

Davies, Gwendolyn, 10–11
deindustrialization, 7, 14–17, 55,
139–44
Deliverance, 125–6, 132
Desmond, Viola, 7, 145n2,
149n1
drug abuse, 20, 118–19, 123–35;
opioid crisis, 124; prescription
drugs, 118–19, 123–35

Each Man's Son, 33–8; coal mining in, 33–6; environmental determinism in, 33–6; environmental issues in, 37–8; masculine body in, 33–5; Scottish culture in, 33–6. *See also*
MacLennan, Hugh
Echoes from Labor's Wars,
26–33; class in, 31–2; coal mining in, 26–33; the extractive gaze in, 33; masculinity in,
30–1; memorialization in,
26–30; oral tradition in, 29–30;
sacrifice in, 27–8. *See also*
Fraser, Dawn

Ferguson, Michelle, 127–8
Fitch, Sherrie, 146n4
folk paradigm, 12–14, 20, 29, 50,
55, 92–3, 99–100, 125
Fraser, Dawn, 22, 26–34, 37–8,
43, 68, 146n1; *Echoes from
Labor's Wars*, 26–33
Fuller, Danielle, 145n4

General Mining Association, 54,
56, 60
Giardina, Denise, 135–6
Gibbs, Terry, and Garry Leech,
69, 143–4
Glace Bay, 8, 22, 50, 53, 83,
119–20; in *Cottonland*, 129–35
Glace Bay Miners' Museum, The,
42–4.
Goin' down the Road, 37, 147n3.
See also Shebib, Donald
Greer, Darren, 111–15; *Just
beneath My Skin*, 111–15

Hage, Ghassan, 17–18
Halifax, 21, 42, 88, 112, 116;
in *Poor Boy's Game*, 105–7;
racial politics in, 104–7; in
Trailer Park Boys, 99, 104–5,
107

Harper, Stephen, 10
Hartigan, John, 24, 99, 125–6, 129
High, Steven, 15, 60
hockey, 75–6, 89, 102; in Coady's fiction, 76–8, 81–8
home place, 11, 79, 104, 108, 146n4, 147n2

incarceration; in *Blackbird*, 88–9; in *Poor Boy's Game*, 105–7; in *Trailer Park Boys*, 99–105
industrial heritage, 48–55, 59–60, 138–42
Ivison, Douglas, 79–80, 93–4

Jones, Scott, 118–20
Just beneath My Skin, 111–15. See also Greer, Darren

Kirwan, Amber, 118

Like This, 55. See also McKay, Leo
Lunenburg County, 8

Macdonald, Frank, 65–8, 132, 144; *a possible madness*, 65–8
MacDougall, Angus, 43–4
Mackey, Eva, 75
MacLennan, Hugh, 22, 26, 31, 33–8, 43, 146n1; *Each Man's Son*, 33–8
MacLeod, Alistair, 22–3, 26, 31, 38–43, 68, 70, 98-100, 110–11, 116, 146n1, 147n4; *No Great Mischief*, 40–2
MacNeil, Rita, 25
McDonald, Bruce, 147n3
McKay, Ian, 7, 23, 29, 46, 75, 99–100, 105, 108, 116; *The Quest of the Folk*, 12–14, 20, 29, 46, 93–7; tartan paradigm, 92–7
McKay, Leo, 5, 6, 22, 26, 31, 34, 38, 44, 49, 55–61, 137; *Like This*, 55; *Twenty-Six*, 55–61
masculinity, 10, 22–3, 25, 37, 44–6, 69–91, 148n1; in *The Antagonist*, 84–8; and class, 20, 69, 84–5, 106–7, 142; in *Each Man's Son*, 33–5; in MacLeod's fiction, 38–40; masculine body, 29, 33–5, 37, 45, 77–88; in military imagery, 27–8; in "Play the Monster Blind," 77–9; in politics, 27; in popular culture, 75; and resource extraction, 20, 27, 38–40, 46, 78, 80–3, 90, 113; and sacrifice, 20, 25, 45; in *Saints of Big Harbour*, 79–83; and sport, 33–5, 77–89, 106; in *Trailer Park Boys*, 103–4
Mean Boy, 71. See also Coady, Lynn
memorialization, 8, 16, 18, 22, 48, 51, 54, 64, 66–7, 69, 137; in Clark and MacDougall, 42–6; in Fraser's poetry, 26–33; in *Twenty-Six*, 58–61
Men of the Deeps, The, 25
Mian, Sarah, 6, 94, 107–16; *When the Saints*, 94, 107–11
Mi'kmaq people, 34, 54, 69, 94, 97, 110–11, 114–15, 144
Morton, Erin, 146n7

Newfoundland, 11, 31; literature of, 11
New Glasgow, 118–20

Nixon, Rob, 31, 122
No Great Mischief, 40-2, 98. See also MacLeod, Alistair
Northern Pulp, 17, 146n10
nostalgia, 6, 32, 70, 96; and deindustrialization, 15, 121, 129, 139-44; in Nova Scotian literature, 13-15, 22-3, 32, 38-9, 60-1, 63-5, 100-11, 115-17; and resource extraction, 27, 46-7, 54, 90, 113, 121; in *Trailer Park Boys*, 100, 103-4
Nova Scotia Museum of Industry, 6-8, 49, 51, 54, 59-60, 138-42

oil sands, 55-6, 69, 122-3, 143-4
outmigration, 10-11, 20, 124, 131-2
Oxyana, 24, 120, 129-35

Pictou, 7, 23, 48, 96
Pictou County, 7, 16-17, 54, 96, 118-19, 144; in *Twenty-Six*, 55-61
"Play the Monster Blind," 77-80; male body in, 77-80, tourism in, 77. See also Coady, Lynn
pollution, 5, 9, 16, 19, 22-3, 51, 100-11, 138; and drug use, 119-24, 130, 132, 135-6; in *Tarcadia*, 63-4
Poor Boy's Game, 105-7. See also Virgo, Clement
possible madness, a, 49, 65-8, 132, 144; pollution in, 65-8; postindustrial decay in, 65-6; rehabilitation of the landscape in, 66-8. See also Macdonald, Frank
prison industry, 16, 50-1, 146n9

Quest of the Folk, The, 12-14, 20, 29, 46, 93-7. See also McKay, Ian

regionalism, 9; in Atlantic Canadian literary criticism, 10-12; relationship with masculinity, 90; stereotypes, 9-10, 12, 14, 92-3, 99, 125, 136
resource extraction, 13, 17-19, 25-6, 37, 69, 139-44; extractive gaze, 28, 33, 57, 60
Richards, David Adams, 23, 70, 146n9
Romney, Mitt, 72.

sacrifice, 22-3, 37; and coal mining, 27-8, 53-5, 44-5, 70; in Fraser's poetry, 30-3; and masculinity, 25-6, 40, 90-1; and memorialization, 28-9, 46; in *Twenty-Six*, 57-60
Saints of Big Harbour, 79-83, 93-4 144; class in, 82-3; ethnic tensions in, 83; folk culture in, 93-4; male anxieties in, 79-83; sport in, 80-3. See also Coady, Lynn
Scott, Rebecca, 16-17, 28, 51-2, 57
Scottish culture of Nova Scotia, 10, 20, 23-4, 56, 116; in *Each Man's Son*, 33-5; Gaelic language, 56, 61, 95-6; in *Glace Bay Miners' Museum*, 42; in *a possible madness*, 67-8; in *Saints of Big Harbour*, 82-3, 93-4; in *Tarcadia*, 61-3; tartan paradigm, 95-100
Shebib, Donald, 147n3; *Goin' down the Road*, 37, 147n3

Sobeys, 54, 101, 126, 137, 144;
  Sobeys Industrial Monument,
  54, 137
Springhill, 7–8, 16, 21–2, 48–9;
  Miners' Museum, 6, 50–3;
  Springhill Bump, 52
Stellarton, 3; as Albion Mines,
  34, 66, 56–61; Foord Street,
  27, 54, 60, 137–8; in Leo
  McKay's fiction, 56–61, 137;
  Miners' Memorial, 27, 30, 54;
  mining in, 8, 18, 138–9
Strange Heaven, 71, 79, 126.
  See also Coady, Lynn
strip mining, 3, 8, 14, 17–18,
  54, 126, 138; in *a possible
  madness*, 67–9
Sugars, Cynthia, 98
Sydney, 7, 15, 18, 21–3, 52, 30,
  119, 129; in *Tarcadia*, 61–5
Sydney Tar Ponds, 18; in
  Tarcadia, 61–5

Tarcadia, 49, 61–5, 67; class in,
  64–5; industrial landscape in,
  62–5; Scottish culture in, 61–2.
  See also Campbell, Jonathan
tourism, 3; in *Cottonland*, 125;
  dark tourism, 43–4, 50–5; as
  economic strategy, 6–8, 15, 46;
  and folk paradigm, 10–14, 17,
  92, 128; in *The Glace Bay
  Miners' Museum*, 42–3; in
  "God's Country," 44; impact
  on literature, 9; and industrial
  heritage, 6, 16, 18, 21–3, 42–4,
  48–55, 57, 60, 69, 139, 144; in
  "Play the Monster Blind," 77;
  in *a possible madness*, 66–8;
  and Scottish culture, 10, 23,
  95–7; tourist gaze, 57, 60, 92;
  in *Trailer Park Boys*, 102;
  in *When the Saints*, 109
Trailer Park Boys, 6, 20, 70, 92,
  94, 99–109, 111, 114–15,
  126–7, 132, 146n9; consumer
  culture in, 101; family in, 103–
  5; landscape in, 101–3; nostalgia in, 100, 103–4; racial
  politics in, 103–5; service
  industry in, 100–2
Tremblay, Tony, 9
Trump, Donald, 27, 72, 116.
Twenty-Six, 5, 21, 26–7, 44,
  55–61, 64, 67, 144, 147n1;
  extractive gaze in, 57–8; industrial heritage in, 58–61 in relation to *Echoes from Labour's
  Wars*, 26–7; Westray disaster
  in, 56–61. *See also* McKay, Leo
2016 presidential election, 72
2012 presidential election, 72
Tynes, Maxine, 107

Vaughan, R.M., 12–14, 89, 144
Virgo, Clement, 105–7, 116; *Poor
  Boy's Game*, 105–7

Westray disaster, 3, 7, 54, 137;
  demolition of silos, 3–5, 138;
  in *Twenty-Six*, 56–61; Westray
  inquiry, 7
Westville, 8, 17
When the Saints, 94, 107–14,
  116. *See also* Mian, Sarah
white trash, 20–1, 24, 99–100,
  116–17; in *Cottonland* and
  Oxyana, 129–35; and drug use,
  119–26, 136; and the folk paradigm, 92–4; in *Trailer Park
  Boys*, 100–5; in *When the
  Saints*, 107–11

Williams, Raymond, 18–19, 64, 67–8
Winter, Michael, 11, 23, 70
Wright, Eliot, 138–42
Wright, Liz, 138–42
Wyile, Herb, 10–14, 20, 55, 69, 92–3, 99, 125